The
Wild Birds'
Song

by Jim Coplen

Hiking South on the Appalachian Trail

American Bison Publishing Company
South Bend, Indiana

Printed and bound in the U.S.A.
First printing October 1998

For information contact: American Bison Pub. Co.
PO Box 6784, South Bend IN 46660-6784

Library of Congress Catalog Card No. 98-96689

ISBN 0-9667137-0-2

Dedicated
to all those who dare to act on their dreams

Acknowledgments

My deepest appreciation goes to Connie, who sustained me with encouragement and support during the entire journey. I could not have made it without her.

I thank Kim Owens, who showed me the sometimes error of my ways in putting together the manuscript for printing, and all the people around me—friends and family—who kept me going when times were bleak.

To Karren Cooper, who gave freely of her time and wonderful editing abilities, I owe a debt of gratitude that can probably never be paid by either word or deed.

THE FIRST STEP

I stood 5,267 feet above sea level with gale force wind wailing and stuttering out beyond the huge, broken outcroppings of rock that formed this mountain the Indians called Katahdin. Far below, in a sea of green, reflected light from rivers and lakes dotted the landscape of Northern Maine. Mist-shrouded ranges extended in all directions as far as I could see. Somewhere down there was my future.

For a while I wondered what I was doing on that cold, barren summit. Was this really where I belonged, 1,100 miles from my home in Indiana and the security of a newspaper editor's desk? I was 58 years old, an age when most men were gearing down for retirement, not pushing their bodies and minds beyond anything ever attempted when younger.

More than 2,000 miles of mountain trails awaited me once I descended Katahdin and took that first uncertain step that followed the path into the trees. I pondered uncertainties yet thrilled at tomorrow's discoveries. Surely I wouldn't miss ringing telephones or gridlock traffic on hot summer days; nor any other distraction of urban living. Ahead lay new surroundings I had only read about: solitude in deep forests; high summits and pure sunlight in open places. And all that distance to go.

Fully knowing my life was about to change, but of my own free will, I turned then and began walking south toward Georgia.

Chapter One

South Bend IN to Penobscot River ME
June 4-June 9

"The first accident occurred when I slipped in a fast rushing stream..."

Veteran hikers will say the only way you can train for the AT is by doing the AT. If I'd heard that before 1995 things might have turned out a lot differently. By the time I found the statement to be a truism, however, it was way too late to do anything about it.

When I first learned of the Appalachian Trail from a story in Reader's Digest long ago, I was impressed with the thought of such accomplishment. The story was one of immense challenge: a solo hiker making her way along an incredible distance, over mountain trails and through all extremes of weather. Though I fantasized briefly about doing it myself one day, the possibility seemed remote. How would I find the time for something so involved? How could you plan something like that, and where did your planning even begin? There were obviously more questions than answers so the trail became a distant memory of someone else's adventure while I went on about the business of everyday living.

A few years ago, when I realized my physical condition was giving way to gravity, I started doing more serious hiking—walking at state parks mostly.   But I increasingly liked doing more miles and began thinking about extended trips.   That's when I remembered the Appalachian Trail and started doing research.   Just out of curiosity.   I still wouldn't actually have the time for it.   That was my safety net, the thing that kept me securely at home—not having the time.

Then I suddenly left my newspaper job in February, '95, and thoughts of the trail erupted full-blown into my consciousness.   One thing I had learned in getting older is that we all make enough compromises in life—putting off things we'd rather do in favor of what's expected.   But I finally realized I didn't want to play the "what if" game any more. What if I had just taken the time to do this or that when I was younger, before I became too old to even consider it?   So with a certain independence from both career obligations and pressing financial needs, I decided there might be nothing to stop me from walking the Appalachian Trail except myself.   After that realization, the idea of actually hiking 2,158 miles with a pack on my back became both intimidating and exhilarating.   It's one thing to think idly of adventure and a different matter to actually plan the attempt. Suddenly, the daydream had come closer to reality and my pulse rate went up a couple of notches.

I gathered more information about the trail a piece at a time, just to see how far I would get before abandoning the goal as just too much for this old body to handle.   The trail, I learned, is marked with 2x6-inch white blazes, painted mostly onto trees, and when above timberline, onto rocks. With endpoints in Maine and Georgia, it passes through eight national forests, six other units of the national park system, and about sixty state park or game lands.   It leads hikers through Shenandoah National Park in Virginia and the Great Smoky Mountains National Park in Tennessee.   It is the longest continuously marked trail anywhere, and though a mere 70 years old, the mountain chain it follows is among the oldest in the world, having been formed 450 million years ago by the collision of drifting continents and later defined by glaciers.

As I brought together maps, books, and other materials, the venture began to take on the chilling feel of inevitability.   Nearly every time I sought information about the trail it appeared, in either old back issues of magazines or in a book I randomly pulled from a library shelf. It became like pieces of a jigsaw puzzle falling slowly but surely into place. It began to seem almost preordained. I eventually introduced the subject first to my wife, and when she failed to talk me out of it, to other people. Doing that, I fully knew, placed me in the position of having to go ahead with my plans; as though speaking of the idea aloud gave it form and substance.

While growing up on a farm, walking through woods and fields was something simply enjoyed, though its appreciation was not then so clearly defined. Then when I began canoeing several years ago, I found in quiet streams a rhythm and peace I had misplaced, and the feelings of youth and middle-age were joined in a love of the outdoors I have since vowed to never lose again.

In 1993, I canoed the 210 mile length of the St. Joseph River near my home, completing it over a period of nine consecutive Sundays in spring and summer. As adventures go it may have been a tame endeavor, but it started me thinking that other things were possible—like an extended journey along a mountain chain in the rugged outback of Eastern America.

Since I knew next to nothing about camping equipment, I studied catalogs, hiking guides, outdoor magazines, everything I could find that might provide information in gathering what I would need for the trip. My main concern was to keep pack weight as low as possible, believing the less I had to carry the better my chances of not wearing down in the early stages, before building up body strength and stamina. Cold foods were chosen, eliminating the need to carry a stove. The food selected was summer sausage, Colby cheese, beef jerky, pita bread, and a mixture of walnuts and raisins. I would need quite a lot of it initially for the 10 to 12 days it takes to travel the first section, called The Wilderness. I included a can of sardines just for an emergency, but decided it was too heavy and left it at a shelter early in the trip.

Outside Baxter Park, The Wilderness section occupies roughly 100 miles of trail, beginning at Abol Bridge and ending near the small town of Monson, Maine. For its entire length, there is very little possibility of leaving the trail to reach habitation.   A few old approach roads are available at times, but beyond that the signs of civilization are limited to mostly fishermen who have flown or bushwhacked their way in.   No telephone or power lines, no pavement, no homes; just the occasional hiker staggering onward.

For weeks at home I made jerky and collected food supplies when they were on sale.   I packed them into bags, then different boxes, their size depending on where and when I could get to a post office along the trail.   Fifteen towns were chosen for mail drops—places either on the trail or near enough that I could get into town and pick up a package from home.   All the boxes had been prepared with pre-addressed labels and numbered by order of shipment.   A master list indicated when they should be sent, according to mileage estimates formulated with the help of trail guides. Twentyseven pounds of the nut/raisin mix and several rolls of waxed cheese crowded a spare refrigerator.   I was proud of my organization.

I bought a bivy shelter because it was the lightest tent I could find.   The bivy was barely big enough to cover one sleeper, but weighed only two pounds, four ounces.   The sleeping bag was summer-weight, also under three pounds. An outfitter advised me well on boots, and for that I am eternally grateful.   I learned later that if your feet give out because of ill-fitting boots, the rest of you isn't going anywhere either.   The clothes I chose to take were a mishmash of mostly cotton materials because I thought they would be light and cool.   As I became a little bit trail-wise they were replaced with more intelligent choices.

I did not plan to stay over at many towns but keep hiking in order to finish in four months or a little longer.   Optimistic, but doable, I thought.   After all, there would be about 16 hours of daylight for hiking during the peak of summer. My mileage plans soon became a lot more flexible.

As I prepared for the trip, my walks gradually became longer and more frequent.   I scrambled up the steepest hills I could find nearby, then about a month before target date began wearing my new pack loaded with about 20 pounds of books and miscellanea.   It felt strange at first but the time would come when that pack was like a second skin;

a natural part of my body that made me whole when I carried it. Gradually increasing the pack weight to about 28 pounds, I walked longer distances, ending with an 11 mile hike from my home to the park and camping overnight. Walking home the next day I felt fairly satisfied with my conditioning. I planned to walk about that same distance each day through The Wilderness. True, the mountains were missing from my practice hike, but at least I thought I had an idea of what I could do.

The majority of those attempting a thru-hike of the AT—that is, end-to-end—begin at the southern terminus of Springer Mountain in Northern Georgia. By doing so, they can take advantage of warmer weather and begin as soon as early March, though most start in April. Those northbounders then have the pleasure of following spring as it comes first to Georgia, then Tennessee and North Carolina. They see more flowers bloom and the grass turning green, before summer finds them in Virginia. Mount Katahdin, for them, then becomes the climactic finish to their long journey if they make it there before October 15, when the trail to the mountain's summit is closed to travel.

For northbounders who fall behind schedule and fear they won't make it to Katahdin before the cutoff date, "Flip-flopping" becomes an option. The term refers to leaving the trail, probably in New Hampshire, and traveling to Maine to climb the mountain, then hiking south to where the trail was abandoned; thus doing a thru-hike, but not in a strictly continuous fashion.

Traveling south, I decided, would allow more time for planning, between February and June. I would also have more room in most shelters, I supposed, and if I was still on the trail late in the year—well, at least I would be in the southern states. Then too, I was seeking a measure of solitude which I was afraid wouldn't be possible among the 1,200 to 1,500 who started north each spring. Another factor, I realized later, might have been a rebellious instinct to go against the normal flow. The terrain in Maine and New Hampshire, I learned, would be the most difficult of the trail. But once I got past that I would be well on my way and, hopefully, ready for anything ahead.

Most southbounders don't begin until after May, when

weather conditions are more favorable in the north, so early June was chosen as my kickoff from the summit of Katahdin at Baxter State Park in Maine. I just wasn't sure how I would get there. Travel to Baxter is difficult unless driving direct. I found Amtrak and airlines go to Boston or Bangor and from there a bus can be taken to Medway, 10 miles from Millinocket, the nearest town to Baxter. Getting to Millinocket is another problem, and from there it's another 20 miles to the park. A taxi is available however, and hitchhiking is always an option.

While checking airline, bus, and train fares, trying to finalize my plans, a friend told me she could schedule a planned week's vacation to Cambridge, Massachusetts around the time I wanted to leave, and her brother would drive us from there to Maine. We left South Bend on June 4, and arrived at the brother's apartment in Cambridge on the 5th. It proved to be a relaxing time, exploring the area that included historic Boston, eating steamed clams at Fanueil Hall, and anticipating the coming months.

On the evening of the day before the three of us were to leave for Maine, I became ill with diarrhea and vomiting, and blamed it on the clams. I was empty and dehydrated, my system purged as though prepared for a new beginning at the start of the trail. I was definitely feeling shaky, but it would have taken something a lot more serious to hold me back. Anticipation was at a peak.

Driving up took my mind off illness. The scent of pine needles and ancient decaying layers of time; the sight of all those lakes and streams; the looming mountains—they would soon be the everyday trappings of my new life.

It seemed a long way just from the front gate of Baxter Park to Katahdin Stream Campground, where I'd stay the night. I enjoyed the trip but was anxious to be near the starting point of my odyssey and thought we'd never get there.

I tried a show of nonchalance as we explored the area of the campsite, then my two companions wished me luck and left me with my uneasy thoughts—and a 34-pound pack that felt a lot heavier. Suddenly, I was alone in a remote, forested section of Northern Maine. The traffic lights were gone, the stores, the police, ambulances and hospitals—

everything I had once relied on and took for granted. The idea of tackling the Appalachian Trail just then seemed nearly overwhelming. It was a big, rugged country out there. My heart beat a little faster at the thought, my mind contemplating the dangers, my soul somewhat committed to the challenge.

The shelter was 3-sided, made of logs, with an open front and a wooden platform for several sleeping people. Similar, I would find, to shelters all along the trail. The breeze was cool and pure, like a clean, pine-scented perfume, and I inhaled deeply.   Densely-packed trees surrounded the site, the only sound was of birds and a gurgling creek passing perhaps 60 feet away.   Above and beyond the trees to the front, Katahdin loomed mysteriously, a gigantic, rounded mass of rock projecting itself into the sky.

My friend had given me a large book for company and I read from it that evening, but left it for the park rangers next morning.   I couldn't pack that two-pound tome into the Maine woods, no matter how good it was.

I didn't sleep much that night.   Temperatures dropped into the 30s and I shivered in my light bag, wearing just about all the clothing I had with me, including thermal underwear and a down vest.   I was getting an early lesson in the vagaries of mountain-country weather.

June 9—I woke at the first hint of light (Katahdin is the first place in the U.S. to see the sun), dressed—or rather undressed—for my climb up the mountain, stowed everything else into my pack and walked to the ranger cabin across the creek, where I knew I was allowed to leave my pack. Because the terminus of the AT is actually at the summit of Katahdin, marked by a sign stuck into a rock cairn, southbounders must first climb the mountain to begin. They then come down by the same trail they went up, so it's a great relief to be able to leave their packs at the bottom and start the long trip free of extraneous weight.

After signing the register at the ranger station, I began the 5.2 mile walk up Hunt Trail with just some water and an extra shirt in a plastic bag.   The time was 4:55 am, the sky clear, wind fairly calm among the trees of the lower approach trail that my guide book said would lead to the summit.

For a long distance creek water, high from snow melt,

became thundering cadence among the densely growing spruce and fir, in a rush to reach the bottom. A deer crashed into a brief opening among nearby trees, leaving only a glimpse of white tail.

I was energized with excitement and probably intimidated by the mountain, so I hurried. Consequently, time passed quickly as I climbed the trail that became gradually steeper, changing from grass and dirt to loose rock and roots. Rocks soon became boulders and the exertion it took to overcome them made me sweat even as cold winds found me in the higher, exposed areas.

Past Thoreau's Spring, where the path began to level near the top, above treeline, there were stretches of boulder fields. Small, isolated patches of snow clung in shaded places; iron bars were implanted into rock faces, to pull myself up and over. I remember few other details of the trip. Perhaps I should have savored it more, but over 2,100 miles of trail lay ahead and I hadn't yet learned to slow down and appreciate my surroundings. I may have been driven to haste by the fear of failure. If I couldn't make it up this mountain, if it proved too difficult for me, then the trip ahead was only an illusion.

At the end of the upward trail, I reached the place that has become either the beginning or finish for over 3,000 thru-hikers since the AT's opening in 1937. About 90% of those completing the trail begin in Georgia and see Katahdin from a long way off, pulling them onward. Others, like myself, have chosen to begin at the most difficult point, using Katahdin as an impetus for following the Appalachian chain like a river flowing south, toward the sea.

The entire area was gray rock, reminding me of photos in National Geographic of the Mongolian landscape, or perhaps of the Russian Steppes. Another trail, Knife Edge, extended like the rippled back of a dinosaur below and beyond the top of Katahdin, linking it with other peaks. That walk along a narrow path in the open, blowing air above clouds seemed inviting, but not so much as the trail I must now retrace to the foothills. I touched the wooden sign with carved letters that said I had reached the northern point of the Appalachian Trail and implanted the moment forever on my mind, knowing I would want to recall it in other years.

Turning then and walking quickly back the way I'd come, I met others going up, including two young men who said they were also thru-hikers.   I said I would probably see them somewhere later, not really knowing if it was true. Others I saw only from a distance.

I was first off the mountain by several hours and returned to the ranger cabin at five minutes after noon to collect my gear.   I should have been tired but adrenaline still drove me. The way ahead seemed more open to discovery somehow, hidden in shadow instead of prominently displayed on a mountain's face, and the trail inside the park was a controlled area.   Only by being outside the boundaries would I feel I was truly on my way at last.

I'd been curious about how the trail would actually look; how large, how easy to find? The path ahead, twisting and turning through deep pines and birch, was narrow. Wide enough in most places for only one hiker, but soft underfoot in the level forested section before the mountain chain really began.   In places the trail was worn deeply enough into the forest floor to follow without the white blazes I'd seen painted on rocks, and now on trees bordering the trail, but often it seemed to merge with game trails and required concentration.

Walking toward the Daicey Pond campground, still inside the park, where most hikers spend their first night after climbing Katahdin, I overtook a father-and-son team. They too were attempting a completion of the trail, they said, but were obviously having serious problems already. Overloaded with equipment, the teenage son was angrily struggling to maintain balance while the father was doctoring already blistered feet. The boy's pack, I was told, was too big for his body, and so he was forced to carry most of its weight on his shoulders instead of on his hips in the manner for which modern packs are designed. The grimness on the two faces as I passed made me want to help, but I knew of nothing to do, and was frankly relieved that I wasn't in their position and might survive the first day myself. I never saw the two again and assume they were the first dropouts I would meet.

After the mountain, that first day's walk was fairly level, along a park road, past ponds, and over makeshift bridges that spanned streams somewhat precariously. For the wider expanses I found my own way by wading the shallows, then hopping from rock to rock in the deeper sections.

The first accident occurred when I slipped in a fast rushing stream and fell face-first onto a large rock as I struggled for footing. I was wet only up to my hips and had just a little blood on my nose, but realized this was going to be a learn-as-you-go experience and the miles hard-earned.

As I entered the dense forest beyond the park boundary, I suddenly felt remarkably at peace. This was where the journey really began and I was doing it. There was no feeling of needing to do anything else.

Near evening of that first day I camped along the Penobscot River, having walked 17 miles. My bivy was set up among trees 100 yards back from the water. I ate very little and blamed the lack of appetite on lingering effects of the clams. I was happy just to be there—actually on the trail, heading into a future with purpose. As I lay in the gathering darkness, uncountable images of the day flickered past my closed eyes, crowding out most other memories: my scramble up the intimidating mountain and down again; onto the trail and past the security of the park, to this place where I was entirely alone, enveloped in the silence of the trees, far from home. It all seemed a dream even before I slept. And outside it all was the excitement of a completely new day awaiting, certain to be unlike any I had ever lived before.

Chapter Two

Penobscot River ME to Long Pond Stream ME
June 10-June 18

"...all I could do in any case was struggle on, over the next mountain."

During that first night along the Penobscot River in Maine I was awakened suddenly by the sound of thundering hoofbeats. Though the noise became increasingly louder and the animal seemed headed directly for my tent, there wasn't much I could do except hang onto my sleeping bag and pray. The noise fortunately detoured left at the last minute and I was spared being found in a bivy shroud next morning, victim of a rare moose trampling. Here I'd fallen onto the rocks while crossing a stream the day before, and now had almost been run over by a large wild animal. Quite a start, I figured, to whatever it was I was doing.

Heard another moose that morning, crashing through the brush as I walked along the river. I had driven to Maine not many years before in search of wild moose but found none. Now I was at least hearing them.

I missed several turns in the trail that second morning. Finding myself on paths that became smaller and fainter, I backtracked until seeing white blazes again, then tried to keep them in sight ahead of me. But often the blazes were either faded or far apart and not easy to follow. If it was going to be like this all the way, would I be able to find my way? I had thought the trail was going to be easier to see. The general goal, I'd heard, is to have blazes no more than one-quarter mile apart, but I learned that because of a shortage of volunteer maintenance workers in remote sections, that is not always the case.

Near Abol Bridge a red fox darted from the trees and crossed the road ahead. Next day a gray fox would leap from the trail into tall grass as I approached. Seeing wildlife was a joyous thing for me.

At the bridge I encountered my first trail store, the only one until Monson. It was a small convenience shop with gas pumps and quick-shop items. Such places would always be oases along the AT—welcome stops for hungry, weary hikers. After coffee and a brief rest break, I took one last look at those scanty signs of civilization—there wasn't even a telephone there, but leaving the store behind was like letting go of my last bit of real security—and crossed Abol Bridge. I was officially into The Wilderness and on my way at last.

All along the AT, in varying ways, markers are placed to inform the hiker of approaching shelters and frequently, of important intersections. Most often, the mileage from shelter-to-shelter is given and helps to provide a sense of timing. Then too, *The Thru-Hiker's Handbook*, which virtually all hikers carry, also denotes distances along with other useful information, such as how to get to nearby towns or stores. As a sort of ritual, we tore pages from the book when they were no longer needed, as a way to further lighten our load, albeit in a small way. The discarded paper was often useful in starting fires.

The path was still level, traversing the low ground until a little over three-and-a-half miles later I came to Hurd Brook Lean-to. My guide book listed 227 official shelters conveniently scattered along the AT, and in general design there are probably as many variations of them as there are states that touch it. Most are built of peeled logs, but often of stone, cement block, or boards.   They are usually three-sided, with an open front, approximately 12 feet long, 8 feet deep, and 7 feet high, with a wooden sleeping platform about 2 feet off the ground. Sometimes there are large, wooden pegs, but mostly it's just large, metal spikes driven into the walls, both inside and out, for hanging packs and other gear. All lean-tos, I would find, except for the newer ones, came replete with the funky odor of long-on-the-trail hikers and their often wet equipment.

At the lean-to I encountered another hiker with problems. The young man had developed knee trouble, he said, and had been there several hours trying to recuperate enough to walk back to Abol Bridge so he could get into better shape before trying again. Once more there didn't seem much I could do but sympathize, and anyway felt he was in no imminent danger. I never heard of him again and suppose he was unable to restart the trail after all.

So far, in my first two days of walking, the only people I had met on the trail were apparent dropouts, and we hadn't even gotten to the mountainous section yet. That thought filled me with concern if not outright dread. And yet the realization that I was still moving forward had to be a positive point, I rationalized.

At Hurd Brook I wrote my first comments into a trail register (something about this being my second day, and admitting to my uncertainties). At almost all shelters a notebook of some kind is left for hikers. They can enter the date of their visit, comments about the trail, notes to others, or whatever philosophy they want to leave for posterity, and usually signed with a trail name.

For the last several years it has become traditional for thru-hikers to take trail names, chosen by either the hikers themselves or bestowed by others as a reflection of some personal quirk or trait. Before leaving home for Maine I had taken a six-iron from an old set of golf clubs to use for a walking stick. I used "Six-Iron" as a signature at that first shelter and it would be my identity to others as I hiked the AT. Most people I met out there were known only by such names, as though with the old life left behind, new names were necessary to start over.

Later that day, while continuing to walk mostly through bog country, I met my first northbound hikers. The father-and-son team of The Norwegian Fireman and Bigfoot had been section-hiking over the years and were just then on the last part, with Katahdin their end-goal. They smiled as they talked about the final miles and I naturally offered congratulations. I was happy for them and also for me now that I'd finally encountered other hikers who were making a success of their trip. I'd begun thinking my own walk would be a lonely one if I survived, because everyone I'd met up to then seemed to be getting off the trail.

That same afternoon the land began to slope upward and I encountered a stretch that seemed extremely tiresome and difficult, making my legs ache and causing many rest stops. Thinking of it weeks later I realized it was only a bump in the landscape compared to almost everything else to come.

In my tent at a campsite that evening, just before dusk I heard the familiar sound of hoofbeats again, but this time coming at a walk. I was more curious than scared this time as I raised to watch the bull moose stroll through camp 20 feet away. Slightly less curious than I, he merely glanced my way and continued toward the nearby lake. His antlers seemed immense—trees growing from his head. I would find the reaction from moose to be varied: they seem either very frightened of humans or ignore us altogether. And they apparently liked hiking the AT themselves because we found large piles of "moose nuggets" on the trail throughout Maine and into New Hampshire.

Somewhere during my second day of hiking I'd begun to notice a sore left knee and by the third day it was too painful to put much pressure on. It especially troubled me walking downhill, and I concluded I may have gone too far and too fast that first day, beyond my limitations. It was hard to tell, though, where our limits lay, and knee problems would plague most thru-hikers at varied times and places along the way. Ace bandages, while not particularly stylish, became common attire.

Being forced to slow down, I walked only four miles on the third day, arriving at Rainbow Stream Shelter early in the afternoon. A soft, cool rain fell later, as other hikers arrived.

Shortly after I settled in, a young lady and two young men stopped for lunch and protection from the weather after hiking in from a nearby logging road. They were interested in my proposed thru-hike and the girl invited me to call her sister and brother-in-law when I got near their home "just off the trail" in Vermont. She thought they would be happy to provide help if I needed it. Such invitations would become part of the magic of the Appalachian Trail; virtual strangers asking us into their automobiles and homes, presumably because they saw us simply as people needing help. In retrospect, I think they also wanted to touch on the experience we were going through, to become part of our "great adventure".

That evening I also met the hiker who would later adopt the trail name Avi Maria. He too had climbed Katahdin on the 9th, but had stayed at Daicey Pond Campground that night. Avi offered me hot tea—the only thing that had tasted good to me in a long time—and made an instant friend, though I would not see him again until Monson.

Another male hiker arrived after Avi and last to come in that day was a young lady carrying one of the largest packs I have ever seen. She was not frail but staggered beneath the weight and, unbalanced, picked her way slowly down the rain-slicked bank to the stream crossing. Reaching the shelter at last, she dropped her pack onto the platform and lay beside it, gasping. In later conversation she proclaimed herself a thru-hiker but we all knew she was off to a bad start. Included in her evening's meal supply were heavy canned goods, and other things we saw were bulky and heavy. I would guess the entire weight at about 60 pounds. Others tentatively offered advice that would help lighten her load, but she discouraged further attempts at such talk.

Even though I slept fitfully, the sounds from Rainbow Stream were restful that night. Such backdrops would become a part of trail life, but the soothing, calming effect of rushing water occurred less often once I was out of New Hampshire.

Because of the painful knee I left late next morning, but others were still at the lean-to, among them Big Pack. Her situation seemed hopeless and I later learned from The Dixie Boys that she was still in her sleeping bag at 9:30 that morning. She disappeared from future trail news, perhaps having taken the logging road out to civilization.

Although I didn't realize it at the time, I was becoming dehydrated during The Wilderness section of my hike. My mouth and throat seemed continually dry and at night it was difficult to swallow. Later, with the wisdom of hindsight, it seemed I should have known to drink more water. But I suppose there were so many other details to attend to I simply neglected one of the basic hiker rules. I would learn in time how important it was to properly interpret each pain or discomfort—to decide what was important to my survival and ambitions, but in the beginning everything was a mad mix of signals coming from all directions. Then too, I may have been distracted by the continued lack of appetite, which obviously could lead to bigger problems if not corrected. At intervals I literally forced the dry, cold food down my throat. The dehydration, of course, made that more difficult and I often gagged during the attempt.

At first I wore long cotton pants and cotton tee-shirts during the day, while walking, and came to realize my choices for clothing were not altogether good ones. I saw what others were wearing and we talked about new, lightweight synthetics available from suppliers. I also began wearing shorts when I found how much heat the body generated while hiking.

The light sleeping bag I had chosen proved out in the long run. While it left me chilly on the coldest nights in the mountains, pack weight was daily becoming the most important consideration among serious hikers. We talked about it in shelters the way parents talk about schools for their children.

While I was content with the solitude of deep forests and remote mountain peaks, there would be times when I craved the company of others. By starting alone on the trail I'd hoped I would have the best of those two differing worlds, and so far it was working to my satisfaction. My third day on the trail I saw the two hikers I'd met on Katahdin the first day. They were calling themselves "The Dixie Boys" collectively, but individually they were Screaming Eagle from North Carolina and Howling Dog from Mississippi. Both had just graduated from Mississippi State University and decided to hike the trail while deciding what to do with the rest of their lives. I found that to be a common theme for younger hikers, and for ones my age it may have also been a transitional period, only of a different kind.

Until I walked into Monson I saw The Dixie Boys almost daily, but mostly walked apart from them. We often occupied the same shelter at night and discussed our individual progress, took stock of each others' equipment and supplies, and discussed the terrain ahead as though there were anything we could do about it but keep walking.

The uphill angles seemed to increase daily, to the point where I found myself gasping for air on steep vertical climbs and began seeing the world from higher viewpoints. Frequent rest breaks, though brief, provided a chance to lift my eyes from the trail and drink in the beauty of the landscape I was passing through. But at one point my eyes were not watching the right place at all. While making my way down the bank to cross a stream I slipped and fell against a broken branch, making a three-inch tear in the skin of my right leg, near the knee. I stopped later long enough to wash it, and applied iodine. This new wound was only a small part of my new medical history. Not long before I had found a pain in my right foot, just behind the big toe, but at least the new injuries took my mind off the sore left knee.

On the fourth day I limped to Wadleigh Stream Lean-to, just over 38 miles from Katahdin, and walked 10 miles the next day to Potaywadjo Spring, past Nahmakanta Lake, through bog country again where trail maintenance workers have built wooden pathways for hikers. Peeled logs split in half were connected end-to-end with the flat section on top. Those makeshift bridges often extend hundreds of feet and while a welcome sight just above the water and mud, become slippery with rain, making the footing treacherous. I think every thru-hiker has fallen from at least one such span. I took a header from one later down the trail and walked the rest of that day with muck-stained pants and the stench of swamp hanging to me.

In Maine, bridges across rushing streams are uncommon, at least along the AT. Usually the fording place is at a shallow crossing with rocks strategically placed for use as stepping stones. At first I waded barefoot with boots slung around my neck, icy water making my toes stiff as they tried for a grip. After Monson I wore rubber-soled sandals for traction until sending them home to lighten my load again.

At one fording site, the water, whipped into foam around

boulders and bends, was too deep for stone-hopping. A log had been positioned in the stream for those daring enough to walk it, but even with long sticks in each hand I felt it would have taken a spectacular balancing act, bobbing as it did on the water. With a pack to unbalance me, I wasn't about to make the attempt. Instead, I left my boots on and plunged into the hip-deep water, waist belt unfastened so I could shed the pack if I went under, and used the log as a guide, pulling myself across and through the water. The boots had been wet anyway, from rain and damp grass, so they merely squished a bit more as I walked.

I walked often in wet boots, mostly soaked from rain and heavy dew that clung to tall grass and ferns and found its way past the waterproofing. It became habit to hang them at night from the top rafter of a shelter to dry. That also kept them from porcupines who reportedly savor the taste of salt contained in human sweat.

It was hard to tell at that point if things were getting better or not; everything seemed a strain. I was beginning to believe that hiking The Wilderness was about the most difficult thing any human could do, and asked myself over and over again why I was doing it. But by then I was at the halfway point of that section, and supposed it was as easy going forward as back.

My sixth day on the trail took me to Cooper Brook Falls in a cold rain. My right ankle was then being rubbed raw by the stiff leather collar of my boot, but a chronically sore back I'd had since September of the year before had cleared up. I attributed that to the fact I carried no sleeping pad, lying instead on the hard wood floors at night. Perhaps, I mused in half-sleep, there were going to be tradeoffs when it came to discomfort.

That day I'd seen a small, dark shape coming toward me from the ferns that grew along the trail, and not knowing what it was, stepped aside. I saw then it was a grouse who undoubtedly had a nest nearby and was warning me away. For a small bird her silent attack was pretty intimidating, with feathers all ruffled and wings poised like weapons, so I detoured several yards, giving her a wide berth.

I was still not eating much so left part of my food in the woods for animals, knowing they would find it more appetizing than I. There was no use carrying it into Monson; more was expected there in a package from home and each ounce of weight was taking on huge importance in my belabored mind.

Next day brought the steep uphill section where all southbound hikers earn the layover in town. This was decidedly becoming the mountainous Maine of trail lore. I made 11.6 miles, mostly in cold rain, to Logan Brook Lean-to near the summit. I wrote in my journal that evening: "I need different clothes, and better food."

On the eighth day I saw bear scat on the trail. Went only a few miles to Newhall Lean-to, but up and over four mountains that included the towering White Cap (Boy, was this thing getting steep!). The day was sunny and I had time in the afternoon to dry my clothing from a line at the shelter. Dry clothes had become my "poor man's luxury," and made getting up in the morning just a little easier.

On the early part of the AT in Maine I was usually awake at first light, around 4:30. By getting an early start I was able to take breaks throughout the day and still get into a shelter early enough to relax and take care of my gear; to dry out wet clothing if the sun was out. By getting there early I was also pretty sure to find space at the lean-tos whenever hikers became bunched up on the trail.

Arrived at Chairback Gap Lean-to after 10 rough miles in an intermittent drizzle the ninth day. I had walked briefly through an area called The Heritage with eyes toward the sky as white pines suddenly towered into the mist. In colonial times shipbuilders came from the coast to this area to choose trees for masts on their sailing ships. Innumerable layers of dry needles softened the path and gave off a musty odor to mix with the ever-present scent of fresh pine, and I much too soon passed from the area.

I still had no appetite but the knee seemed better. I think there were three mountains that day but I may have lost track. Every step then seemed the most difficult thing possible, and doubt began to occupy my thoughts. I occasionally questioned, not my commitment, but my ability. Perhaps I had started too late after all—not in this one year but in all the years of my life. Yet all I could do for now was to struggle on, up and over the next mountain.

Stringing a clothesline to a tree in front of the shelter that evening, I turned to see a cow moose headed my way. It's a given that moose in Maine have the right-of-way, but there wasn't much room to maneuver as I stepped behind the tree and she passed on the other side. I could easily have touched her as she ignored my presence and ambled away. Later another moose strolled through camp as I watched from the safety of the lean-to. Snowshoe rabbits, with their strange, huge hind legs were brave enough to come near in search of food scraps.

While most animals were a welcome sight to me and I wanted to see bears if at all possible, I didn't want them near me in darkness. To help prevent that, "Bear Poles" were present at many shelters on the extreme northern part of the trail where hikers could secure their food bags at night. Several dozen feet from the shelter a metal pole extended perhaps 12 feet from the ground with an umbrella-like arrangement of bars extending from the top at right angles. A separate pole with a hook hung from the array and could be used to lift the bag upward, where the drawstring was looped over one of the extensions and left overnight. That seemingly frustrated both the hikers who craved a late-night snack and hungry marauding bears.

I did 10.9 miles on Sunday, the 10th day, ending with a hard climb over Barren Mountain to Long Pond Stream Lean-to. I met two middle-aged women there who were section-hiking The Wilderness area. They were fun and interesting, sharing hot tea and asking questions about my own hike.

As would happen all along the AT, I was asked about my peculiar walking stick, the golf club. After I had explained its presence, one woman laughingly suggested I had hit a ball from Katahdin and was now chasing it down the trail. That scenario planted the germ of an idea that would lead to a continuing saga I wrote into trail registers the rest of the way, about the mythical ball I was chasing. Often, hikers I passed on the trail would comment about the club, then ask such things as: "Did you lose your ball?" or, "Hit a bad slice?" I would usually respond by telling them about chasing my initial drive to Georgia if necessary, and for a little while we had something to distract us from ordinary aches and pains.

That evening, at the shelter, I also met Start One, a young hiker just graduated from high school. He described his own trip as "...a rite of passage," a time of solitude to organize his thoughts and plan his future. The theme was common for many of differing ages, I was to find, only most of us didn't yet have the wording quite figured out.

Two young women later came into camp struggling with heavy packs. After setting up their tent they stopped by the lean-to and we learned they were walking The Wilderness to raise money for charity. They had come only a few miles their first day, not being prepared for the trail's difficulty and we could see the strain they were under, having gotten pledges from donors and now feeling some pressure to continue. When the girls learned I was going south they asked about Barren Mountain and the other terrain ahead, but I could only smile and shake my head. Walking that section had left an indelible impression of how nearly impossible the trail could be and my pack was a lot lighter than either of theirs, still I didn't yet feel confident enough in my own abilities to be giving advice. I felt bad for them as they groaned at my silent response and retreated into their sleeping bags.

I could hardly wait for morning to come. Monson was only 15.3 miles away but over a gentler and kinder landscape, the guide book promised, so I was determined to make it in one day. Having been on the trail 10 days fighting cold rain, bogs and bugs, steep mountains and cold nights, I was as ready as I would ever be for rest and recuperation.

The Dixie Boys had gotten ahead of me but I knew I would catch them at Shaw's Hiker Hostel in Monson. Like me, they were anxious for a hot shower, clean clothes, and a soft bed, in almost that exact order. The only variation for them was of food. For me that particular craving was to come later.

A typical trailside lean-to

Chapter Three

Long Pond Stream ME to Little Bigelow Mountain ME
June 19-June 24

"I heard men shouting, 'Jason! Jason!' and asked if they'd lost a Scout."

I left most of my remaining food supply at the shelter when I departed Long Pond Stream Lean-to early in the morning and later learned that another hiker had made use of it. My goal was to reach town yet that day and the way things were going I would need little if anything to eat along the way.

The ten days of The Wilderness had been a mixture of discovery, pain, awe at my surroundings, and some confusion about future plans. I was tired, dehydrated, and worried about my lack of appetite. At Monson I hoped to sort out those problems and find answers. The place had begun to take on great significance for me; somewhere to settle in and get my bearings, so to speak.

After crossing Long Pond Stream soon after leaving the shelter I could find no more blazes marking continuation of the trail, but finally located an old roadbed that seemed headed in the right direction and followed that until the blazes reappeared. The trail then turned right onto a larger dirt road, but I saw no markings again for a long time. A woman at a house assured me I was still following the AT though, so I plodded on under an increasingly hot sun until reaching a paved road. Unsure then of where to go I asked directions at a nearby campground, but they were unable to help, so crossed a bridge to another road, believing it led in the general direction of town. By then I had given up on finding the trail, supposing I had lost a turn somewhere.

I soon flagged down a van and the driver offered a ride after confirming the road would take me to Monson, eight miles away. I declined her invitation, thinking that if I walked in it might make up for being off the trail. The purity of my intentions soon gave way to solid reality.

Like any other trail hiker I've known, I would come to detest detours onto pavement. Because of pack weight, hard road surfaces pound the entire body, and there usually isn't much shade. After two or three miles of plodding under a baking sun (The temperature for that area, they would later announce, was a record-breaker), I slipped off my pack and dropped beside the road beneath a tree, wondering why I hadn't accepted the van ride. Minutes later a flatbed truck stopped alongside and the elderly male driver leaned out the window to announce in a Yankee drawl, "I think it's too hot for walking today."

Not wanting to make the same mistake twice, I concurred, and after we strapped my pack onto the truck bed he drove me to Monson while telling me about all the other hikers he'd given rides to over the years.

When we pulled into the driveway of Shaw's Hiker Hostel I knew immediately it was the place for me. Hikers passed in and out of the screened back door while others busied themselves cleaning or sorting gear. Though I still had over 2,000 miles to go with many other stops along the trail, nothing would ever seem more welcome than that homey old building. Filled with food, beds, and other hikers who came to be family, it had become my only salvation, I felt. I definitely had problems, and if not for Shaw's my trip might have ended short of New Hampshire.

For northbounders Monson is the last stop before Katahdin and trail's end. For southbounders it's welcome relief after ten or more days of hiking, long before they've gotten their trail legs after just 115 miles. The reality of the long walk stretching before them has probably sunk in by then and it's time to take stock of their ambitions. Still, at no other place along the trail will it be so far between towns, and most find renewed hope in that simple fact.

I began drinking cold liquids upon arrival, just after signing in, and continued until the dryness left my mouth and throat. I still wasn't sure why I hadn't drank more water on the trail from Baxter Park. There was enough available but I simply don't remember being very thirsty. The problem may have been caused by overall excitement, but I believe my body just hadn't yet adjusted to the sudden changes thrust upon it.

At Shaw's I was reunited with The Dixie Boys and Avi, and also met Q-Tip and his dog, Max, Little Engine, The Grazer, The Tennessee Walkers, Wandering Jack, and Hummer, all headed south on the AT. For several months, I would continue to see many of the hikers I had met at Shaw's.

The Shaws operate out of a main house where the family lives, with private rooms for rent and a back room serving as the hiker's lounge. A washer and dryer are available in the lounge area and a bunkroom upstairs has a number of beds. Additional bunks are available in the barn behind the house. I paid $15.00 per night for bunkroom space and paid extra for morning and evening meals.

After much-needed showers, a complete washing of clothes, and good food, we mostly spent our time conditioning boots, sorting and repairing equipment, patching blisters, and discarding items we felt we could do without. Most of our loafing time was spent discussing gear, trail experiences, and what to expect up ahead. Otherwise, hikers continually drifted in and out of the building, going to the store, post office, or restaurant. It seemed we all just wanted to confirm the idea of having all those signs of modern convenience nearby.

The food was abundant with basic meat and potatoes, more than one kind of vegetable, home-baked bread, and iced tea and coffee. Knowing of my condition the Shaws all but force-fed me. My plate was piled with food I wasn't sure I could handle. When it became likely I would someday see the bottom of my plate they added more. They served, I shoveled. It must have been what I needed because two days later my appetite was nearly back to normal.

At Monson I sent home heavier clothing and phoned an order for lighter-weight gear to a popular supplier. They promised delivery to the Caratunk General Store three days away. I also called my wife, Connie, and told her to suspend the shipment of food boxes, except for special occasions. The cold food theory just wasn't cutting it. From there on I would depend mostly on buying my own food in an effort to both lighten the pack weight and improve my menu. By studying a trail guide it appeared there would be no more than four or five days between available stores most of the way, so I felt I was making progress on the supply side of my trip.

Wandering Jack said he was beginning his fifth thru-hike on the AT, this time with his teenage son, Hummer, who would have to return to school in the fall. I asked Jack why he kept coming back to the trail and he said because each time was different. That puzzled me because I'd already seen just how strenuous it could be, but the time would come when I understood his compulsion. I assumed he'd learned a lot over the years by trial and error, so asked a lot of questions. Then from Shaw's hiker store I bought dried meal packets, a stove, sandals, and more appetizing snacks, replacing the heavier foods I'd planned to eat cold.

The thing I hadn't been able to replace though, was my six-iron walking stick. When I'd left the truck that took me to Shaw's the club was missing from my gear, and I realized it must have been left in the grass along the road where I'd rested. It may have been possible to go back and find the club, but I was never really sure of where I'd been at the time I lost it. In light of how much time was expended in trying to find another one, though, I probably should have tried to find that place.

Instead, Keith Shaw, owner of the hostel, drove me around most of Tuesday afternoon, to antique shops, flea markets, and sporting goods stores in neighboring towns, trying to find a replacement club. But I could find only complete sets and really didn't want to play the entire course between there and Georgia.

By then I had grown quite fond of the club as a useful tool. Holding it by the blade on downhills, I was able to set the rubber-tipped handle onto the path ahead of me as a brace. It even helped on uphills by providing a sort of balance, and when walking the flatter areas of land the metal shaft slid smoothly backward into my hand, held loosely there, in rhythm to my walking. All those actions had become fairly automatic by the time I'd reached Monson so that the thing had begun to feel a part of me. It had also become a tag that other hikers recognized, a symbol to me of who I was and where I was going.

By Tuesday evening it looked like I might have to leave next morning without my golf club. Those at the hostel sympathized.

Just before dark that last evening in town, Screaming Eagle, one of The Dixie Boys, decided to go walking by the local swimming hole at the river, and seeing something in the grass reflecting the last light, bent to see what it was.

I was inside the lounge later when I heard a voice calling me. Outside Screaming Eagle handed me the eight-iron he'd found there by the swimming hole, and said, "Here, you're back in business."

I had changed two numbers in club length but the difference in walkingstick quality would prove to be negligible. The story of the golf club became one told to other hikers up and down the trail, so that when meeting later many said they had already heard of me. For those who hadn't heard the story I would feel it necessary to explain why Six-Iron was carrying an eight.

Two days before Monson, Screaming Eagle had developed knee problems and limped into town ahead of me. During his stay at Shaw's, after a telephone discussion with his doctor, he decided to leave the trail and let his knees heal. I never saw him again but he had become an indelible part of my own trail history.

I left Monson Wednesday morning, June 22, with the lone survivor of The Dixie Boys, now calling himself simply, Dixie. After the rest, hydration, and abundance of food, I felt the same enthusiasm as that first day on Katahdin. My body seemed healed; I was renewed with confidence, brash enough to have sent my mother a postcard stating: "There ain't no mountain I can't climb now."

The trail was mostly flat that day and we cruised, ready to stretch our legs after confinement in town. The miles passed in a poetic rhythm as we quickly found our stride. Went 18 miles to Moxie Bald Mountain Lean-to, anxious to see what lay ahead. I saw my only black bear that morning, a blur as he crashed through the underbrush about a hundred yards to our right. The trail then curved and he must have crossed ahead, beyond our line of sight, because we heard more noise on our left and assumed it was the same bear, but didn't see him this time. He seemed more afraid of us than we were of him. I later found that that fear of humans was the major difference between park bears farther south and their more wild cousins of the Maine woods.

We walked a long time along the Piscataquis River, with two fordings. The water rippled over varicolored stones in sunlight and cooled hot feet as we waded in sandals through the shallows.

The Tennessee Walkers, a stepfather/son team, and a friend, had arrived at Moxie ahead of us, having left Monson the day before. They already had a lot of gear scattered about the lean-to when we arrived, so Dixie and I put up tents near the lake.

We then learned the friend had met with an accident that afternoon. He'd been wading in the lake and opened his right heel on a sharp rock. The wound was serious enough, they felt, to need medical attention. The area was quite remote but fortunately there were other campers nearby, and one with a canoe offered to take the injured hiker across the lake and leave him at a roadway near a fishing camp. They assumed someone would be along from the camp soon and take him to town. I never felt it was cruelty to have left him there—it was the only thing to do really. Each of us knew the risks we faced going into those remote areas and did what we could to help, but our options were always limited.

The man with the cut heel had also become sick in The Wilderness. When I arrived at Monson he and his friends had already been there several days awaiting test results. They'd suspected Giardiasis, a diarrheic condition often caused by drinking water polluted by animal feces. It seems most prevalent in streams flowing from beaver ponds and everyone seemed aware of the danger. Most hikers treated their drinking water, but it's doubtful anything will prevent the illness if you're one of those susceptible.

The man's tests had proven negative, but whatever the reason for his illness he now seemed accident prone after his mishap in the lake. I later learned the group made it as far as Gorham, New Hampshire, but that one of them had more problems and they left the trail, vowing to try again later.

The next day began with a climb up and over Moxie Bald Mountain and included another across Pleasant Pond Mountain. According to maps, a lot more of the same lay ahead. But with some problems solved I became more aware of my surroundings: the path was most often a tunnel lined with caribou moss and white birch trees against the thick, dark green of balsams, red pine, spruce, and fir. The sun was a distant, sometimes flickering thing that bloomed suddenly and lit the graveled bottoms of shallow streams and clear ponds when we broke from the forest cover.

The trail required constant attention in order to make our way safely. Roots projected from the ground where the topsoil had been worn away by countless other feet and the broken, sometimes sharp rocks were to be avoided or used carefully as stepping stones. A thumping sound echoed almost constantly from our boots as they bumped against the rocks and roots, blending with sounds of the forest.

Small, red pine squirrels were everywhere, chirping birdlike as I trespassed their world; seen from a distance, sitting on a log or ancient tree stump, twirling a pine cone between their paws like an ear of corn, eating the seeds that lay between layered petals. The petals flew and often built into great mounds to show later where the squirrels had fed.

At a lake we caught up to Avi, who had also left Monson before us. Later, one night in camp he told us he had come to the trail because of a speech he'd heard given by one of the ex-hostages in Iran. The moral behind the speech had apparently been to not put off those things that could somehow improve the quality of one's life. Avi had graduated from the University of Connecticut the year before and spent the intervening time at a job he felt was going nowhere, so he heeded the advice he'd heard and left to go hiking.

Sitting in a leaky old boat he'd found on shore, with a

rotting board as paddle, he was trying to catch fish from a line he'd fastened to a tree branch, but having no luck.

I had seen that small trout were fairly easy to catch from streams that ran by shelters. Many hikers carried hooks and line, and rigged poles with bugs or worms as bait. Fresh fish grilled over an open fire in the wilds of Maine would be something to remember but I carried no line or hook until later when another hiker shared his supplies with me.

On Thursday Dixie, Avi, and I made it to Caratunk, a town even smaller than Monson. But it was near the trail and had allowed us to carry only a three-day supply of food getting there. The place consisted of a small general store with a post office inside. As would always be the case at towns along the trail, we were like greedy children in a candy shop. It was there I discovered the hiker's fondness for Ben & Jerry's ice cream.

My package of new clothing ordered in Monson wasn't waiting for me as I'd expected. The catalog supplier was supposed to have addressed the box to me c/o General Delivery Caratunk, but it was sent UPS instead. As with any such package mailed to post offices along the trail this one was marked "Hold For AT Hiker", so the driver had an idea I might show up at the store, where the post office was located. That meant I had to wait around several hours for the driver to arrive on his return circuit. Meanwhile Dixie and Avi continued down the trail.

Ferry service across the nearby Kennebec River operated free of charge to hikers from 10:00 am to noon daily, but I didn't leave Caratunk until 3:00 pm. After a phone call for special arrangements, I met the ferry operator at the river 20 minutes later, anxious to catch up.

The wide and sometimes angry Kennebec is often forded by more daring hikers, but the day I crossed it the water level was unusually high and I would probably have had little chance making it on my own. I knew that in 1987 a woman hiker drowned there when the current pushed her over and the pack held her down.

The ferry was actually a canoe, and a paddle was provided me so I could help with the work. It was an enjoyable change of pace, using different muscles to crosscut the current before gliding to a predetermined site on the opposite bank.

Time slowed as a falcon glided across the river valley, above the forest as we drifted at the end. But I hurried when reaching the far bank, scrambling up the slopes to higher altitude. Before dark I needed to reach Pierce Pond Lean-to, where the others were planning to stay.

While some shelters are located next to the AT, most are along side trails marked with blue blazes, and may be as much as a mile away. In my rush I completely missed the lean-to sign but didn't realize my mistake until a mile or so beyond. Signs pointing out a shelter's location are not always obvious and hikers, their eyes mostly on the trail, can easily miss them.

Rather than backtrack to find the others, I continued walking as the ground had become level again, passing among pine groves with a ground cover of soft, fallen needles that eased my sore feet. Considerable daylight remained and I was making better progress than planned so I continued to a stretch of overgrown roadbed about three miles from Pierce Pond where I camped.

Next morning I built a small fire and burned some of the heavier cotton clothing I'd been carrying, replaced by what I'd picked up in Caratunk. At the store I'd stuffed the new package in on top of my other supplies, but the time had come to lighten my load.

I stopped at West Carry Pond Lean-to for lunch next day and let the others catch up. By the time we reached Roundtop Mountain the terrain had taken a turn for the vertical and it was often necessary to either pull ourselves onto rocky ledges by clutching small trees or by holding onto the rock above as leverage. On one such shelving, while struggling for footholds, a branch caught my glasses, flinging them backward onto the rocks below. I turned and watched horrified as they bounced from one level to another, waiting for them to shatter. But they soon caught and held. I lowered my pack and retraced my weary steps 50 feet, pleased to learn they had suffered not a scratch, but did not enjoy redoing that part of the climb.

Walking alone an hour later, I was in the lead at the foothills of Little Bigelow when I was surprised to hear shouting ahead, and came to a Boy Scout in uniform, about fourteen, chin quivering. While hiking with his troop he had become separated, he said, and assuming they had gotten ahead, had followed someone's advice to run to a ridge down the trail and begin shouting. By the time I saw him he hadn't found the other Scouts but had attracted the attention of two men doing a road survey nearby. Having lost his canteen during the panic run, the boy was thirsty, very hungry, and frightened.

I told them I was certain the boy's friends weren't down that part of the trail as I'd just hiked several miles from that direction and hadn't seen them. The surveyors then volunteered to take the Scout back to their truck parked on a nearby road and give him food and water. I advised them to stay at the road so I would know where to direct the others if I found them.

A half-hour later, as I struggled up Bigelow in the intense heat, reflecting on how quickly my "cruising" days were over, I heard men shouting, "Jason! Jason!," and asked if they'd lost a Scout. They admitted, reluctantly, they had, so I told them where he could be found. They then asked me to stop at Little Bigelow Lean-to where they'd left the remainder of the troop and fill them in on current events.

I'd planned a night-stop at the shelter anyway, so had time to visit with the scouts and answer questions about my thru-hike while they packed their gear in preparation for leaving. After they'd gone, I had the shelter to myself and rested awhile before heading to The Tubs nearby. Reflecting on past events, I thought, this has been a pretty good day: a rescued Boy Scout and a salvaged pair of glasses. About the only thing I had to regret lately was the statement, "There ain't no mountain I can't climb now." I was definitely having doubts about that.

Chapter Four

"My body absorbed more punishment than I thought possible..."

The Tubs are depressions in a stream bed formed between the walls of a natural rock sluice on Bigelow Mountain. Water gathers in the depressions, before its final downward rush to lowland, and the neck-deep pools help wash away the pain and weariness of passing hikers. I took all my clothes that needed cleaning and let them soak while the cool water washed over me. For a while it had seemed debatable whether risking my naked body clambering down the steep walls would be worth the results, but it was.

Dixie soon arrived, then Q-Tip and Avi. Q-Tip and his dog, Max, had hiked with the two women, Little Engine and The Grazer, since Katahdin, after meeting them on the trail. Just past Caratunk however, he pulled away and joined us to make a foursome.

At that time Q-Tip actually had no trail name but would soon become known as Wrong Way Willie, or simply 3-W, because we caught him heading north from a shelter one morning and had to turn him around. The name never really stuck though, and later at Hanover, New Hampshire, when he told us he saw his reflection in a store window and thought, "God, I look like a Q-Tip," he had found a new trail name. Tall and slim, with a mop of perpetually uncombed hair, he certainly looked the part, and would remain Q-Tip beyond the end of the trail.

He is from Alabama, and like Avi, had graduated from college the year before, but worked for an outfitter at Jackson, Wyoming before deciding he needed a new direction. That direction turned out to be south from Maine.

Next day the going was difficult so we covered only 7.4 miles, making the interminable climb up Avery Peak to admire the sunlit view from a wide, rocky bald. From there we could see all the mountains we would have to climb for the next few days.

Saw another moose that day but he was running away from a lake in early morning, toward deeper cover.

We climbed West Peak the day after, then The Horns, and Cranberry Peak, before entering Stratton, Maine in near perfect weather. We had already decided to stay overnight there for some rest. It was eight days since I'd left Monson, nineteen days since I'd climbed Katahdin, and it often seemed to have been longer ago. So much had happened already, each day new; so many changes taking place both in my body and in the way I saw things.

For one thing I was drinking water again and most minor ailments had cleared up. I no longer felt the next stop might be my last.

We stayed at a motel in Stratton that catered to hikers. The owner, a hiker and all-around outdoorsman himself, seemed to enjoy our company. That may have been part of the reason we decided to stay an extra night. During one of our casual conversations he initiated the idea that Ben & Jerry's should add a special flavor to their ice cream line just for hikers. We adopted the quest as our own and decided the name of the new taste treat should be "AT Crunch." Later I wrote up a petition on note paper found in a shelter, asking the Ben & Jerry's people to consider a request of the undersigned for AT Crunch development. I further asked that they consider including blueberries to represent Maine and pecans for Georgia, and that although ibuprofen was an ingredient requested by others, I didn't think the FDA would approve its inclusion. I would then explain the petition to those I met on the trail and ask for signatures, hoping to gather a respectable number of them before the trip ended.

I resupplied in Stratton with enough food for five days— next stop Andover. We'd been hearing a lot about the Mahoosuc Range just ahead, leading to the White Mountains. We were warned it would be the most difficult part of the trail. At the end of almost every day, lying semi-comatose in the shelter, I felt as though I'd just done the hardest part. Again. So I was more than a little overwhelmed with the threat of the Mahoosucs looming.

Little Engine and The Grazer caught up with us our second day at Stratton. I admired the courage of the two women on their own taking what the trail threw at them, just as with everyone else out there. We exchanged gossip over beer and pizza that night and seeing them again was like suddenly meeting old friends you'd grown up with. The distance between us would gradually lengthen as the summer passed, but I would continue hearing of them from others.

My appetite by then was insatiable; my stomach an alien thing, constantly gnawing at the other parts of my body. I became hungry a half hour after eating, thought about food most of the day and awoke during the night thinking about it some more.   I saw our consumption of food as akin to throwing straw into a nuclear furnace. From Monson on that condition would never leave me on the trail and I discovered it to be universal among long-distance hikers. Some estimate that we burned as much as 6,000-8,000 calories daily on average, so food became the main subject wherever we gathered. We compared fixations—as others might compare the opposite sex—but in the end it seemed we liked anything edible with equal passion. Fried chicken, greasy hamburgers, bacon and eggs, milk, and of course, ice cream forever.

I would often wonder at some of the stranger food cravings that overcame me. A lack, I'm sure, in my Spartan diet. At the restaurant in Gorham I found more interest in the bleu cheese dressing than anything else. After the main course I continued eating, like a dessert, the dressing that had come in a separate dish for my salad.

Sometime soon after leaving Stratton I met another hiker coming toward me on the trail wearing long pants, long-sleeved shirt, and a hat with mosquito netting covering his head. He introduced himself as, "Father Time," and asked about trail conditions ahead. Then upon parting, he said, "Well, I'll probably be seeing you in Cheshire, Mass."

At the time I didn't know what he meant, nor did I understand the significance of his trail name. Father Time was the only hiker I ever saw wearing netting to keep the insects at bay. Most of us rubbed repellent onto exposed parts of our bodies, and some brands proved less effective than others. We knew of the danger of using too much and tried to keep its use to a minimum. Then too, after a couple of hours of extreme sweating, most of the repellent had been washed away.

Mosquitoes, black flies, deer flies, and no-seeums were a continual problem throughout Maine and much of New Hampshire. Because I wore mostly shorts, my legs in particular suffered a lot, and Q-Tip, who seemed most susceptible, had his neck covered with bites.

Black flies never seemed to be as bad as predicted, but when mosquitoes were at their worst many hikers chose to put up tents to assure a night's sleep free of their intrusions. I usually just doped my neck, head and hands with repellent, and slept in the shelters.

After some time we observed and discussed a pattern to the mosquitoes' nightly invasion. They seemed to come around just as it got dark and stayed for about two hours. Their buzzing was probably the most annoying feature about them. It seemed that just as you got reasonably comfortable, the slide into sleep was interrupted by the faint, annoying little whine that came nearer with each pass. Curses followed by a slapping sound could be heard throughout the two-hour period they were with us.

The infestation reached its peak at a boggy section of trail in the low country of Maine. We four were separated then, each suffering in his own space. For about a four-mile stretch, mosquitoes were so thick they could be seen as a frightening gray cloud trying to catch up from behind. Comparing notes later we found that each had not dared stop for rest or even slow down. It was then we made our fastest time of the trail, I'm sure. We approximated our speed at four mph; enough to stay ahead of the following cloud and just short of a jog.

We wondered, in the shelter at night, if mosquitoes were territorial creatures. Did they break off the chase eventually, allowing others to take over the pursuit? We warned other hikers they must kill the first mosquito seen at the shelter at night, for he was the scout, and if allowed to leave would then alert the others. With minds freed from ordinary thoughts of modern living, such was the minutiae that filled our time on the trail.

We crossed the Carrabassett River, then Crocker and South Crocker Mountains after a late start from Stratton on Tuesday, and stayed the night at a campsite.

Two days later we climbed The Saddlebacks and getting to the summits seemed to take more hours than a day could hold. The trail there was typical of the entire region from Maine throughout most of New Hampshire and often seemed insurmountable. Steep grades sucked air from the lungs, made knees weak, and the blood pound. I could only walk until my legs became too heavy to move, rest a few seconds, then go on until my body screamed again. It seemed at times the summit would never appear—that there may not be a summit. Walk upward, toward sunlight and hope this was the top of the mountain. But it never was. It was only another turning in the trail and ahead was one more impossible grade.

Boots sliding on loose rock, tripping over exposed tree roots, sweat running and stinging the eyes; pack straps digging into shoulders; knees shaking, chest burning. Finally, when all hope of reaching the top was abandoned, a last lunge and stumbling out of the stunted pines, onto open balds above treeline. And soon, the final, rocky peak above all other false summits I had too easily fallen in love with along the way.

If the day was clear we could perhaps see all the way back to Katahdin. The appreciation for being in such a place was intensified a hundredfold because of the knowledge we'd gotten there only by our own extreme effort. After difficult climbs I might come to an open vista and be able to look back at what I'd just come over, and be amazed and proud at what I'd done. I usually took a rest break there, wringing sweat from my shirt and letting it dry in the breeze while admiring that part of the world spread out before me. In all directions were other mountain ranges fading into blue-gray haze. Somewhere behind—the trail we'd conquered—ahead the unknown and the unforgiving.

If the reward for uphill climbs is the view from on top, then payment is demanded by descent to the bottom. Though easier on the lungs, legs take a terrible beating on downhills. Pack weight drives against the knees, and feet are forced into awkward angles by rocks and roots. If leg problems are going to occur it will probably be on the downhills.

And, inevitably, at the end of any descent on the Appalachian Trail there will be another mountain waiting. I sometimes wailed at a mountain when the climb seemed never to end, or a shelter I looked for at the end of a long day was still a mile or two away. But my outlook changed when I stood above clouds in sunlight, crossed streams that cascaded down mountainsides, or considered life without ever having walked the trail.

We arrived at Piazza Rock Lean-to that afternoon, and with time to spare Avi walked three miles to trailhead and hitched into Rangeley, several miles away. He returned with twelve cold beers, four small steaks, grapes, and a bag of marshmallows in his pack. I grilled the steaks and we had a small feast there in the forest. Later we toasted marshmallows on the campfire until the shelter's caretaker stopped to visit.

The caretaker, whose tent was nearby, maintained a section of trail and saw to upkeep of the shelter. We talked a long time, and eventually he offered to dispose of our beer cans for us. Then he invited us to a personal viewpoint he'd discovered while exploring the area. During the steep, exhausting climb we all questioned the wisdom of such a side trip after an already hard day. But the view and the surroundings made it worthwhile. We stood there at cliff's edge, all of us a long way from home, surrounded by new reality, and watched a falling sun light the final patch of sky like a million campfires slowly dying.

The good food, beer, and extra climbing assured us a

restful sleep in the shelter that night.

The next four days were a mix of steep ascents and downhills; walks over low, rolling hills, and through rain. Over Bemis, Moody, and Hall Mountains. Rain drove away the bugs and mosquitoes temporarily, giving some relief, but we put on wet socks and boots some mornings and walked through humidity that further soaked our already sweat-sodden clothing. We hung damp shorts, tee-shirts, and socks from a line at night in a futile attempt to dry them.

Red efts, small eastern newts in the first stage of development, made their appearance on the trail just after a rain, and had to be stepped over because they moved slowly on their own. I learned they would later metamorphose into water creatures and felt I could relate to their changing physical structure. My body was absorbing more punishment than I thought possible, but seemed to grow stronger each day.

On Monday I began to notice blood in my urine and found the condition lessened after drinking water, so supposed I was again suffering the effects of dehydration. While not worried, I knew the problem would have to be corrected. It was another reason to reach Andover; besides the traditional hot shower, food, and rest.

One of Dixie's knees gave out four miles from Hall Mountain Lean-to and he hitched a ride into Andover. After spending the night at Hall Mountain, Q-Tip, Avi, and I walked six miles to the highway.

I trailed the others and they were nowhere in sight so I began hitching and walking the eight miles to town. Two hours later I had walked seven miles and given up trying for a ride when a man in a pickup stopped, and I rode the last mile.

Andover too, is smaller than Monson, with two or three stores, a restaurant, and post office. We stayed at a hostel in a converted barn, and celebrated the 4th of July. I partially satisfied a longing for fried chicken and ice cream, washed clothes, dried damp gear, and drank all the fluids my body could hold.

We met Missing Piece and Laughing Gym when they showed up later, and the next day Little Engine and The Grazer came in to stay over.

We had joked about having our own parade down the main street of town when we arrived, but settled for a game of horseshoes behind the barn. That night a pair of friendly skunks visited, masking the odor of resident hikers.

Restocked and renewed we left Andover on Thursday, July 5th and I saw another red fox at trailhead. He seemed to be leading the way.

We had come 257.5 miles and had a long way to go but felt like veterans of the trail at that time. Naively perhaps, we all believed that because we had crossed some pretty rugged country, we had accomplished a lot. Getting to Gorham, New Hampshire 42 miles away, though, promised to be at least as difficult as anything we had yet done, and south of that were the White Mountains and the Presidential Range.

I'd been averaging about 10 miles per day getting to Andover and that mileage didn't increase as the trail indeed grew even more difficult.

On Thursday we passed through Mahoosuc Notch, a vee-shaped wedge at the bottom of two mountains choked with a jumble of huge boulders. At some point in time masses of rock must have rolled down each slope to the notch, making passage difficult but interesting for the AT hiker. To follow blazes painted onto the rocks we squeezed around, over, and under boulders, some as large as a small house. Q-Tip's dog, Max, was a trooper, but often had to be pushed from behind or lifted onto elevated ledges. Slabs of ice lay at the lowest points of the notch, beneath the tumbled surface rock. We alternated between intense sweating under a hot sun on exposed treeless crags, and a chilling wind as we forced our way through the shallow caverns.

The notch trip took an hour and beat on us heavily. We had a hard, steep climb out but I was feeling good at that point. The blood in my urine had cleared up and even with the high heat and humidity, the weather could only be described as excellent.

We crossed the state line into New Hampshire that day, July 7, and stopped at the trail marker for photos. It was a milestone; a long way to go for sure, but we looked back on Maine as our "shakedown cruise"—building strength and conditioning our bodies; testing our selection of equipment, and just moving into a certain mindset thru-hikers must reach. All of us, I believe, were developing more of a long-range view of the trip now that we found we could conquer our own feelings and the difficulties of the trail. For myself, I had come to realize that whatever happened to dampen my enthusiasm—rain or pain—each day was complete unto itself and had little bearing on the day that was to follow. At times there seemed no progress, and yet the days and miles would pass, and our expectations lengthened, not just to the next town, or the next mountain, but to the end.

Dixie and I stayed the night at Gentian Pond Campsite while Avi and Q-Tip continued ahead so they could reach the Gorham Post Office before noon Saturday, the next day. The Gentian shelter provided one of the many special views I camped near on the AT. The lean-to faced southwest from an elevation of over 2,000 feet, overlooking a lake in the near distance, bluish-tinted pines framing the picture. Lying in the shelter that evening I listened to the cackling cry of loons, and as reflections of the day faded from the surface of the water, drifted into another morning.

The next day's walk into Gorham was 12 miles long, but mostly gentle slopes down to the valley, so we made good time.

About three miles from town, I met a northbound hiker sitting along the trail with radio headphones around his ears. Seeing me he jumped up and began chattering about bears. I finally gathered that he had met a sow and her cub on the trail, and when they refused to budge he retreated, out of their sight. He was waiting it out when I met him and knew, of course, that the way ahead was now clear and he could proceed. I thanked him for allowing me to be his beacon, wished him well, and hurried on to Gorham.

About noon Dixie and I met Avi and Q-Tip at a motel that had converted a rear building into a hiker's hostel. Since we were the only ones in residence, we randomly chose bunks in any one of several separate rooms along a hallway. Included was a bath with shower, and a kitchen/lounge area with a stove, refrigerator, and television. It was one of the more comfortable places we stayed along the trail. For Max there was also an enclosed porch area, always a consideration when we looked for lodging as a group.

Gorham was by far the largest town yet that we had stopped at. It is spread out along the highway on a narrow valley floor, so getting to stores and restaurants required a lot of walking; something we were used to but not looking for on hard sidewalks, even without packs.

The stove I had bought at Monson required a special type of fuel not always available, but luckily I found it at an outfitters' store in Gorham. I bought two containers there and mailed one to myself at a post office farther ahead, marking it, as usual, "Hold for AT Thru-Hiker".

Wandering Jack and Hummer were staying at a different hostel in Gorham, as were Forest Hamster and others we hadn't met but heard about. We'd been reading Hamster's entries in trail registers ever since Baxter Park and looked forward to meeting him. I believe many of us planned register entries as we walked, which resulted in a lot of creative writing, much of it philosophical. Reading it had become our main source of entertainment because of those like Hamster who found humor or a special insight in our shared condition. More and more, the registers would also be a source of news and communication as we met some of the people behind the names and wondered at their progress.

I resupplied for four days at Gorham, ate all I could hold, washed clothes, and thought about the days to come. When we left the hostel, it was impossible not to notice the hovering White Mountains surrounding Gorham. Clouds usually hid the peaks but we knew we would soon be up there on steep, winding trails at high altitude. From that perspective it seemed a very daunting future, but still there was the excitement of challenge and discovery.

On Sunday, the day before we left, I silently observed the one-month anniversary of my trip. Though I had hardly begun it seemed my whole life had been lived on the trail, or maybe I had simply been reborn there. In any case, having covered almost 300 miles, I still had a long way to go.

Chapter Five

Gorham NH to Ethan Pond Campsite NH
July 10-July 15

"...the storm crackled and boomed, not only above, but around me."

The first day out of Gorham we made low miles after a late start because we'd taken advantage of the Hiker Special breakfast at the motel. That put us into Imp Campsite late in the afternoon where we finally ran into the infamous Forest Hamster.

Hikers pick up news of the trail from shelter registers or when meeting others of their kind in town or along the trail. Everyone is so apparently interested in others' progress or setbacks that it becomes easy to feel you know people out there you've never met. Such was the case with Hamster when we found him. He was simply like an old friend we hadn't seen in a long time.

We exchanged details with Hamster while rolling out our sleeping bags in the shelter, then fixing dinner. Later he expanded on a story we'd heard from others.

Not far out of Monson, Hamster had removed his boots to cross a stream and tied them to his pack. On the other side he found one of the boots had apparently come loose and fallen among the rocks and water, gone for good. Hamster was dead-set against walking in the reverse direction and vowed to other hikers he would not retreat to Monson. Instead, he hiked 30 miles into Caratunk wearing his one remaining boot and a rubber sandal. At the Caratunk General Store, the owner offered Hamster a pair of old boots left behind long before. The boots, though badly worn, were serviceable, and best of all, they fit. They weren't replaced until several hundred miles down the trail.

While hiking together, Hamster and Energizer Rabbit had prepared Bog Reports in the registers for the entertainment of those behind. Among other things, the reports gave mosquito counts and the number of bog logs encountered on any particular stretch of lowland. They were quite meticulous in detail, if highly imaginary.

Hamster just naturally fell in with our group that numbered five when we left the next morning and walked in weather cooler and less humid. Anxious to tackle the Whites just ahead, we planned a long day to make up for the one before (It seemed as though every time we extended our periods of relaxation, we insisted on punishing ourselves for it later).

The White Mountains extend for about 120 miles along the AT, with open hiking on rocky ridges connecting one peak to another above treeline. The centerpiece of the group is Mount Washington, second highest mountain on the trail at 6,288 feet, and the highest in New England. The weather station there once recorded winds of 231 mph. Weather in the Whites, we had heard, can change suddenly—and dramatically. A mild, sunny day often turns foggy, cold, and windy, with the temperature plummeting to dangerous lows. It was for that reason we agonized about what clothing to carry. I still had the down vest I'd started with and long polypropylene underwear from the package received at Caratunk. Light gloves and a knit cap pretty much completed my cold-weather supplies.

Camping is forbidden in most areas of the Whites, and sites would be hard to find anyway unless retreating below treeline, so in case of emergency we didn't want to get trapped between shelters without protection. Too many stories had been told of deaths from exposure.

The trail was a steep descent to Carter Notch Hut. With slippery rocks and ledges, and the ever-present roots to contend with, we searched for handholds and safe places to set our feet. It wasn't hard to imagine sliding off past one of the many turnings in the trail or to feel something give beneath your boots, propelling you headfirst onto the rocks. Going slow by necessity, we arrived at the hut three hours after leaving the campsite, under dark, heavy clouds whipped by a stiff wind. It was obviously going to be a wet afternoon.

The hut system in the White Mountains, maintained by the Appalachian Mountain Club (AMC), consists of eight rather large buildings spaced along the trail and catering mostly to tourist hikers on vacation or weekend walks through the mountains. The huts have bunkrooms, a dining area, and usually a lounge. A fee is charged for overnight stays that include dinner and breakfast. There had once been thru-hiker shelters in the Whites similar to others on the AT, but it was felt the shelters and huts together proved too many impact areas among the fragile mountain plant life, so the shelters were eliminated. The huts become crowded during peak summer months, but we found that most of their crews, hikers themselves, would usually bend over backward to help us.

At Carter Notch Hut, after the crew treated us to hot coffee and leftover cake, we took another look outside and discussed weather conditions. I didn't want to chance climbing out of the notch on slippery rocks, and rain was almost certainly coming. After Hamster and I talked to the hut crew they agreed to let us work off an overnight stay. The others, Avi, Q-Tip, and Dixie, decided hesitantly, to continue on.

Hamster and I spent about two hours that afternoon changing pillow cases and cleaning mattress covers in the bunkrooms with a germicide solution. After that we checked our gear and washed clothes, hanging them inside to dry. A few other hikers showed up later and made their own arrangements for staying.

Off and on throughout that afternoon, cold rain lashed through camp and we knew anyone on the nearby trails was fighting miserable conditions. While we were concerned for the safety of the others, we also felt pretty smug about our decision to stay. I liked it there in that notch, tucked into the foothills, among the trees, with the sturdy wood buildings as security from the storm. It also gave Hamster and I a chance to get acquainted. We found we had at least the one thing in common of both being newspaper journalists. Hamster is probably a dozen years younger than I, and that put us closer in age than most of the others who were a lot younger. He had been working for a newspaper service reporting on one of the presidential primaries prior to coming onto the trail. I didn't ask why the sudden shift in his life but could sense why it might seem the thing to do after the hectic schedule he had probably been following, and the political scrambling he may have been involved in.

Hamster was easygoing, seeming to take everything in stride, so I enjoyed his company. I would find later that our paces were too divergent for walking together a long distance, but such was the quality of most acquaintanceships made along the trail.

That evening, after the paying customers had eaten, we thru-hikers were given leftovers in the dining room. It didn't amount to a lot but tasted better than what we'd been used to on the trail.

The night turned quite cold but we had plenty of blankets and stayed warm enough. Next morning, after a makeshift breakfast in the hut, Hamster and I left the notch. It was a good day under mostly clear conditions, with a hike over Wildcat Mountain that consisted mostly of cresting one summit after another. We became confused as the mountain seemed to have eight different peaks and we never knew which, if any, was the one, true summit.

After Wildcat we began the long descent to Pinkham Notch, one of the most difficult and arduous downhills of the trail. We struggled desperately to maintain balance over loose rock and huge boulders. Switchbacks gave some relief but sweat poured from our bodies as we hurried to make the $5.00 lunch buffet we'd heard about down at Pinkham Notch Camp. Hamster fell behind and I went on with food as incentive.

About half way down I began meeting a lot of young day-hikers headed up. They reminded me of salmon struggling upstream, gasping for oxygen, straining to reach the next resting place. Most asked how far it was to the top and I regretted having to tell them. With a long way to go on already wobbly legs, it looked like any enthusiasm they'd had in the morning was changed to painful reality by noon.

Outside the main building of the complex I propped my pack and golf club against a wall and sat on a nearby bench to rest and wait for Hamster. Pinkham Notch Camp is AMC headquarters in the Whites and attracts a lot of visitors in summer, who drive in over a nearby highway in order to assault the mountains for several days or a weekend. One of them, a young woman sitting nearby, glanced at my walking stick and asked if I was Six-Iron. She introduced herself as Kathy, and said she and her husband, Mike were section-hiking the AT. They had met Avi, Q-Tip, and Dixie the day before, she said, and because they lived near the trail in New York, farther south, had invited the three to call when they got there. Furnishing a telephone number, she extended the same invitation to me.

Soon Hamster arrived and we got inside just in time for the all-you-can-eat buffet—answer to the thru-hiker's prayer. We consumed much more than we had paid for, but I think by then they must have been used to starving hikers. Hamster made one of the thickest sandwiches imaginable, with a half-inch slab of butter, several slices of cheese, turkey, lettuce, tomato, and all manner of odds and ends. That sandwich must have been five inches thick, He seemed proud of his accomplishment as he offered it up for my approval. I gave him his just due, as to any other great artist.

We left just after noon, staggering on full stomachs. At a scale outside the headquarters building I found my pack weighed 27 pounds with full water bottles. A big meal always left me feeling sluggish, and hiking immediately afterward with a full pack was difficult. But who could pass up a feast after thinking of little else for days?

Hamster and I decided on either Osgood Campsite 4.3 miles away or the Madison Spring Hut, another 2.8 miles beyond. It depended on how we felt and how hard the walk was. One thing we knew for sure: it would be a trying day because we were headed for the top of the range where Mount Washington presented a menacing presence.

I pulled away from Hamster again and hiked alone, the trail at first gradual then steeper, but not like Maine. Somewhere along the way I'd realized other subtle changes had taken place: there were suddenly more switchbacks that reduced the degree of vertical ascent but added steps to the trail. The path now zigzagged across the mountain like a broken zipper.

It's easy to become confused by the variety of trails in the Whites and we had to be constantly careful we stayed on the AT which crossed through and around the local trails. More than one hiker has taken a wrong turn only to retrace his steps later; obviously a dangerous move in bad weather.

Just before Osgood, after crossing a stream where a group of women and children splashed in the water, I met my first nude hiker. He was a young man, about seventeen, walking toward me, and it took a moment for the sight to register. Seeing me, he yelped, turned, and ran back up the trail, disappearing in some bushes. When I next saw him he had his shorts on, stammering apologies, saying he had been hiking all day with a chafing problem. His excuse seemed questionable, or at least not very intelligent because of the number of day-hikers in the area. But I only advised him to be more careful because of the family group I'd just passed.

Osgood was deserted, so I had my choice of tent platforms and set up my bivy. There would be no Madison Hut that day. When Hamster arrived he set his tent alongside, on the same platform. During the night I suffered an attack of claustrophobia in my enclosed space and quickly opened the side flap, sucking in air. Perhaps the entire outdoor experience was becoming incompatible with such a confined space. I only know that from then on I had trouble sleeping in the bivy and started comparing the small, one-person tents that would provide a little more room.

The next day, Thursday, at 6:00 am we started up the bare rock slopes toward Mount Madison. From the angles we climbed it always seemed the next peak was the highest, but there were more peaks hidden behind at even higher elevations. It was the White Mountains version of false summits, I suppose. With the views we had it was a mixed labor of love and agony.

Hamster slowed but I continued on, arriving at Madison Hut at 10:30. The building was made of rock and nestled on a plateau, not far below the summit. This way station for hikers operated like the one at Carter Notch, but I had already decided not to linger. I became reacquainted with Start One there, the first time I'd seen him since back in Maine. I was glad to see that he seemed to be doing well. He had arranged a work-for-stay deal the day before and was soon moving on, he said. Hamster made the same arrangement when he arrived a half-hour later, but I wanted to make Mount Washington that day and went on after some lemonade from the crew.

The walk to Washington seemed in slow motion—probably because I could see the towering mountain from such a long way off. The weather was nice—a bit cool with wandering clouds, the landscape majestic in its very bleakness. Sunlight glinted off barren peaks that rose in a broad, open range, unbroken by the large stands of trees seen previously on our trip. Hikers in the Whites either need luck with the weather or must take their chances on high winds and cold, driving rain. Previous visitors had found such conditions to deal with, and many suffered for it.

Most paths along the hills and ridges leading to high peaks were evident, and at times bordered by hand-laid rocks to prevent damage to adjoining plant life. Fragile alpine growth above treeline may take years just gathering strength to make a temporary summer appearance, and one misplaced footstep can virtually wipe it out. In other places the trail was simply blazes painted onto rocks, requiring a constant search ahead as I walked. At the highest elevations, rock cairns had been built as markers to show the path through layers of snow, which can come any month of the year in that area.

I began finding m&m candies periodically along the trail as I neared Mount Washington, presumably fallen from a torn snack bag. I wiped off all I saw, and like Hansel in the forest, ate them while following the path that took me eventually to the summit.

There were day-hikers all over the place and I really began to miss the solitude of the Maine woods. As I trekked down the slopes and up the hillsides I saw the cog railway belching thick, black smoke from a long way off, making its way up to Visitor's Center. Sightseers on the train pointed and took photos of hikers, and people who had driven to the top via the winding road were having their pictures taken around the Appalachian Trail sign as I hurried by.

Inside the Visitor's Center I ran into Start One again, then retrieved a package from the post office with food supplies from home, and went to the hiker's room in the basement to store it in my pack. After a shower I went upstairs for a quick hot dog and soda, but by then had had enough of the overcrowded atmosphere and hit the trail again.

It was only another 1.5 miles to Lakes of the Clouds Hut and mostly downhill. Along the way I caught up to a hiker about my age, but obviously not long on the trail. He turned and saw me approach (Because of the alpine vegetation, the trail in that section is only wide enough for one hiker), but instead of allowing me to pass, chose to stay ahead, slowing me considerably. Irritated, I silently followed, wondering how long the game would last. I walked around when the trail finally widened, muttering a one-word description of his behavior. He had become a distant figure when I later turned to check his progress and I felt strangely triumphant, but then became annoyed at my own attitude.

The crew at Lakes of the Clouds Hut were extremely friendly and allowed me to stay for work. Start One soon arrived and joined me.

That evening, after dinner, I chatted with Start One and others of our kind, and listened to a makeshift band formed by members of the hut crew playing two guitars. Another thru-hiker joined in by keeping time with a set of spoons. The man I'd passed on the trail was there with a large group, obviously day-hikers, strutting about in bright-colored designer gear with high-profile labels, while we lounged about in sweat-stained clothing and rundown boots. There was a distinct separation between the groups. The miles may simply have made us thru-hikers a bit arrogant, but observing the differences, I knew where I wanted to be.

Next morning I swept out the bunkrooms and folded blankets as payment. At 9:30 I left for Mizpah hut; a short hike, but I wasn't comfortable with the idea of passing Mizpah and walking a total of 14 miles along high mountain trails to Ethan Pond Campsite. I expected those miles to come later, with experience and conditioning.

I got into Mizpah early enough to enjoy my stay with a

lot of leisure time. I washed clothes then lay in the sun while they dried on branches of trees. Laughing Gym and Start One both caught up later. Start One's cousin was with us, having come just for the White Mountains section of trail. We all washed windows together that afternoon for our room and board.

The cousin, I would learn, found the trip too strenuous and left a day or two later. I picked up additional news of Start One in days to come. But by the time I reached Vermont he seemed to no longer be a part of the southbound group. The Grazer left at Gorham, planning a return to college that fall, and Missing Piece, who was joined by his sister in the Whites, also disappeared from that section. Anyone not totally committed to the trail will find a reason to leave on any given day, so those would not be the last to go. The farther south I traveled the more it would seem I was on my own, and would learn to appreciate the companionship of others at the loneliest of times.

For the first hour next morning I walked through swirling clouds that surrounded the ridges. It cleared for a time but then drizzled rain off and on. A storm threatened as I made my way across Webster Cliffs. The air was damp and I wore the poncho that covered both me and the pack. I hurried to not get caught in that exposed area where the rocky face of the mountain fell sharply from my right, to trees and a highway far below. But the rocks were slippery from moisture and I picked my way carefully, despite the haste.

A half-hour later lightning and thunder erupted just as I stepped from trees onto the bald summit of Webster Mountain. Since I was the tallest object in the immediate vicinity, I knew it was no place for me—especially carrying a metal walking stick. Retreating back down the trail I walked into the thick pines and squatted, leaning against a tree stump, and arranged the poncho to entirely cover my body.

I like thunderstorms. This one seemed to shake the mountain, making the world come alive. I felt snug and reasonably dry as the storm crackled and boomed, not only above, but around me. The air was just cool enough at that altitude to be comfortable beneath my covering as rain trickled down branches to fall softly, steam rising from the leaf cover. I absorbed the odors of sulfur and wet pine, and may have slept a little then.

After about a half-hour, as the storm began to ease, I heard a noise on the trail nearby and a voice saying, "Hey, how you doing there?"

Before I could answer he continued, "You must be Six-Iron."

I peeled off my covering then and talked to the northbounder who said he'd met Avi, Q-Tip, and Dixie farther south and they had mentioned me coming along behind. I knew the hiker couldn't have seen my face, hidden as I was beneath the poncho, but had recognized the golf club lying nearby.

On the summit again, along an open ridge, I saw clouds being blown by a strong, freshening breeze from around the mountains, through the valleys, and over the tops to disappear in thinning vapor. The sun then streamed through, highlighting first one golden place and then another along the hills and in low places, as other clouds ran before the wind. It reminded me of descriptions I've read of old-fashioned lantern shows: light and shadow—sudden changes of the scenery from a spectacular vantage point.

I arrived at Ethan Pond Campsite early enough to consider more walking, but since the weather had cleared, decided instead to dry clothes. I arranged with the caretaker to work off the $5.00 fee by picking up trash around the camp. The place was crowded with day-hikers using tents but there were only three others in the shelter, a young man and two young women, all section-hikers.

For the time the young man and I were alone and he introduced himself as Pinto, saying he was hiking a short way with the idea of doing the entire AT sometime later. He said he lived near the trail further south and might see me when I got there. His parents then came to the lean-to, having parked nearby, and brought him food. They gave me a banana from the leftover supply, but I would much rather have had some of the fried chicken they gave their son.

I explored the nearby pond I had passed on the way to the shelter and replenished my water supply, then tied up a clothes line. It had turned into a lazy, relaxed sort of day, and with the long rest I was getting I planned an early start in the morning.

Chapter Six

Ethan Pond VT to Mad Tom Shelter VT
July 16-July 30

"...I knew if I was ever going to be seriously injured on the trail, now was probably that time."

After a long rest and early start I walked nearly 14 miles the next day, up and down one mountain to the next in the Presidential Range of New Hampshire, finally arriving at Garfield Ridge Shelter, 3,560 feet altitude. It was already damp when I arrived at Garfield but then a storm blew in. Frigid wind and rain beat through the open front of the lean-to, gusts peaking at about 50 mph. To keep from the cold mist I got into my sleeping bag, wrapped the ground cloth around it and moved far back into one corner.

I was the only one there except for the caretaker, Chris, who lived in a large tent nearby. He agreed to let me work off the $5.00 fee but later waived it altogether. We sat around the shelter a long time talking about the trail and people we'd both met.

By morning it was apparent I wouldn't be leaving for a while. To proceed from there to the climb up Lafayette Mountain was out of the question. Chris came by to check on me and described conditions as "classic hypothermia." Getting caught on an open bald with those winds and temperatures, plus low visibility could be life-threatening, he said.

During that day of July 17, Chris nailed an old tarp to the front of the lean-to, improving conditions considerably. Before that it had been intriguing to watch clouds actually blow into the small clearing atop the mountain and swirl about as though seeking a way to penetrate the shelter. Without much else to do I napped in my sleeping bag on and off throughout the day, ate too much of my dwindling food supply, and caught rainwater from the metal roof so I wouldn't have to splash to the spring some distance away. To say I was restless would be an understatement. The rest was enjoyable but I didn't know exactly where the others were and whether or not they might be moving farther away from me.

In the Whites communications among thru-hikers wasn't as good as most other areas of the trail. While the huts usually had hiker registers, they were often being read by the day-hikers and not available for our use. Then too, direct communications seemed to become diluted from all those other people being around us. Those factors all may have had a bearing on my feeling at loose ends up on Garfield.

By the second morning it was still cool and damp but the temperature had risen and the winds slowed a bit. Having become restless, I took advantage of the break in weather to leave the ridge. Clouds still enveloped me as I walked the remainder of the Franconia Range, mostly above treeline, over Garfield, Lafayette, Lincoln, and Little Haystack Mountains. I wore my poncho most of the morning but the weather steadily improved. It was ten miles from Garfield to the road to North Woodstock, my next resupply point, and I arrived there about noon. Most of the passing traffic was tourists who don't usually pick up hikers, so I walked the additional 5.5 miles to town.

In town I saw Wandering Jack, Hummer and Forest Hamster with an unfamiliar hiker beside the post office. They had somehow passed me and arrived just that morning. The stranger was introduced as Earth from New Jersey. The four were going back on the trail that same day. I was staying overnight so left them and checked into the Cascade, formerly a large private home but now a hiker hostel.

That afternoon, during the usual town chores, I ran into Laughing Gym and we had lunch at a restaurant. Later that evening we met up again and relaxed at a pub. A young man in his 20s, Gym talked to me about his own motivation for walking the trail at that particular time. Like most of us, he too had come to a crossroad in his life and felt he needed time to himself. Consequently, Gym mostly walked alone but was good company whenever we found him.

He later walked outside town to camp for the night while I slept on a softer bed for a change. The next morning, Tuesday, I wangled a ride from the hostel manager's husband to trailhead, and spotted Laughing Gym hitchhiking along the way. We picked him up and he described sleeping along the river. Just about dark, he said, he saw something pass by that resembled a large black dog. We both decided it had probably been a bear and I wished then I had camped with him so that I could have shared in the experience.

Gym and I separated on the trail after getting into our own pace. Though still cloudy, the weather was warmer by then. It was a long ascent up Kinsman Mountain after leaving North Woodstock with some climbing that required use of the hands, then a steep descent down Beaver Brook Trail.

For the second time in as many weeks I observed the phenomenon of hundreds of tiny tree toads, about a half-inch long, littering the trail for perhaps 30 feet. Careful as I might be, it seemed impossible to avoid stepping on a few. At first I tried to walk carefully enough to miss them all, but then averted my eyes and walked quickly through them. I had never seen such a thing and it fascinated me each time.

I went 15 miles that day, leaving the White Mountains behind, and spent the night in open air along a river. Next morning I made the long climb to Beaver Brook Shelter for a rest break prior to the walk up Mount Moosilauke at 4,802 feet. They say on a clear day you can see five states from the summit of Moosilauke, but because of conditions that day visibility was limited to my immediate surroundings.

It remained overcast while a cold wind blew moisture horizontally into my face. I couldn't stop to rest as I normally would when cresting any mountain, or to examine the remains of an old rock hut scattered there, but instead continued onto the descending tree-covered section that offered some protection from the elements.

Conditions improved steadily along with the lowering altitude but the trail seemed to go nowhere. It was undoubtedly one of those down days hikers have. I felt a real lack of progress, pulling my way past sharp outcroppings, stumbling over slippery rocks and roots on sore feet and knees. I fell once or twice but that was nothing new. We all fell on the trail, and the pack weight kept us from catching our balance, often slamming us onto the rocks to lay there dazed and occasionally wounded. The best I could do, I found, was to relax and roll with the fall. Except for one time there was no lasting damage.

I looked for the Jeffers Brook Shelter, only about 9.5 miles from where I'd started that morning, but inexplicably it seemed to be moving away from me. Becoming confused as the white blazes disappeared, I unreasonably began to rage at Moosilauke in particular and all mountains in general as I stumbled down through the dampness, wondering for the hundredth time if I was getting anywhere at all or if the movement of my feet was only hallucination. I soon encountered a blue blaze that always before had indicated a side trail and became enraged at the injustice, believing I had missed a turnoff. To have come so far and lose the way was unthinkable, but I refused to retreat back up that wearisome mountain and pushed stubbornly forward. Eventually, I realized the descent had nearly leveled and saw the trail ahead enter an opening in the forest cover. At that same moment sunlight could be seen over a farm pasture through the opening and the white blazes reappeared on trees. I knew then I was on the right track but never learned why that blue blaze had been misplaced.

After crossing the grassy meadow in clear sunlight, I turned and walked a farm lane along an old rock wall, and my mood was as suddenly changed as the surroundings I suddenly found myself in. I had left behind the most difficult of the Appalachian range and was gradually entering a world of more open vistas and gentler slopes. Many mountains lay ahead but not so much the continuously steep climbs to summits above 4,000 feet.

An early start from Jeffers the next morning and a 14 mile walk in the rain got me to Hexacuba Shelter that afternoon where I caught up with Dixie and Q-Tip. They had stayed the night before and rather than start off in the rain that morning, had chosen to take a day of rest. I was glad to see them and Max again.

Max is a large golden retriever with a friendly disposition. He liked to take the lead with Q-Tip, trotting ahead, only to stop after the trail turned so he could wait until Q-Tip appeared before loping off again. If Q-Tip didn't come immediately into view, Max would head back down the trail until he found him. Consequently, we often remarked how Max was covering more ground than any of us.

Carrying his own animal pack containing dog food, Max seemed like another hiker and may have thought he was. When he hadn't seen me for a while he behaved like an old friend, jumping up to put his paws onto me so he could be petted. Max developed a habit somewhere on the trail that we only later caught onto. Invariably, when several of us slept together in a shelter, someone would awake in the morning with his lower body off the sleeping pad, and the dog occupying the bottom half. It eventually came to light that Max would snuggle against someone during the night until they invariably rolled over, then immediately moved to gain a little space on the pad. He was nothing if not patient and by morning would have taken over the pad an inch at a time. He even pulled the trick on me, even though I slept only on a reflective survival blanket under the sleeping bag. He may have thought the effort with me not worthwhile because he only did it that once.

When Earth arrived later we caught up on trail news and tried to dry wet gear from lines inside the unique six-sided building. Earth fixed me a cocktail of vodka and Crystal Light and talked about the girl from Wisconsin he'd fallen in love with farther back on the trail.

She was a thru-hiker also, who had developed terrible blisters on her feet. Before she left the trail soon after Monson, she and Earth spent time together. Now she was home sending him food packages and he was talking about leaving too. Said he wanted to save a little of his money and buy a truck. I think he wanted something to drive to Wisconsin. I'd met the girl at Shaw's in Monson where she was resting her feet, waiting to see if she could continue, and I didn't blame Earth for his infatuation.

After a long and eventful day, Q-Tip, Dixie and I made it into Hanover, New Hampshire on Saturday, July 22. On the way, atop Mount Cube, I took a nasty fall while stepping off the rocky summit. Planting the handle of my golf club below to provide support, I jumped a short way down to the next level, but in pushing off the club broke through, pitching me forward. With the pack pushing, I felt hurled from a cannon, and as the rocks rushed toward me knew if I was ever going to be seriously injured on the trail, now was probably that time.

Getting my hands in front I twisted to one side as I landed, then rolled once or twice before crashing into a pine tree. Finally gathering enough courage to examine body parts, I found only a few gouges and one large scrape down the front of my right thigh. Although I was sore, everything worked and after picking pine needles from my ears, I was happy just to be mobile and on my way again.

Q-Tip and Dixie were then somewhere ahead and I hadn't seen them in some time. Soon after passing Moose Mountain Shelter, the trail led down to a roadway and I stopped, looking carefully for white blazes on the other side. Finally I saw a metal AT marker attached to a tree but it hadn't been obvious so I felt fortunate I'd seen it instead of wandering off down the road looking for more blazes. After following the trail then for about a mile I saw two figures walking toward me. One crouched to dip water from a small stream, and as I came closer, recognized Q-Tip. The other hiker, I soon realized, was Dixie. Q-Tip looked at me strangely when I approached, and asked, "How'd you get here? And where are you going?"

"I'm following the white blazes," I said. "Where are you going?"

After comparing notes we finally figured out what had happened: when the other two had come to the crossing where I'd looked so long for the marker, not seeing it they had walked about a quarter-mile down the roadway until finding white blazes that led into the woods. Actually, the blazes were coming out of the woods for southbounders. They had unknowingly eliminated a mile and-a-half of woods walking then got back on the trail heading north. It had already been a long day and Dixie and Q-Tip weren't happy about turning around and retracing their steps. "I thought that was you I saw," Q-tip said, "but I was hoping it wasn't."

The trail finally led us to town and we stopped at a frat house of Dartmouth College where free hostel space is given to hikers. Northbounders occupied most of the space, but we spread out on the covered porch and lawn that night after getting settled in. Avi was there, having arrived the day before. Others, including Wandering Jack, Hummer, and Earth, stayed at another frat house two blocks away. Among the group headed north were two elderly Englishmen, but most of them were younger males, excited about having gone that far.

Although Dartmouth College was in its summer session, Hanover bustled with students and people I supposed to be parents of students or simply tourists. Being a college town, it provided just about everything we thought we needed: good restaurants, food stores, an outfitter, and a Ben & Jerry's ice cream shop. I picked up a package of supplies waiting at the post office, mailed home cold-weather gear, bought small items I needed, and ate almost continuously. We intended to stay overnight and leave on Monday but succumbed to what hikers traditionally call, "town gravity," and didn't leave until Tuesday. The pull to stay is sometimes cancelled only by the desire to be back on the trail—making more miles.

The second evening there we walked into a Hanover bar and found a mix of south and northbound hikers gathered. We were a total of 13, some familiar to me but mostly faces behind trail names I had only heard of or seen in registers. We swapped adventure stories until late, like veterans of a foreign war.

Next day the weather was clear and hot walking the highway, then the hills out of town. We looked forward to being in Vermont in just a few miles—I especially. While appreciating the forests and mountains of Maine and New Hampshire, I now looked forward to the farmland of Vermont. They say the AT never gets easy, it just gets less difficult at times. Mountains would continue all along the trail but, relative to what we had already done, they became gradually lower and easier to climb, with more switchbacks.

As usual, Avi surged ahead, while Q-Tip, Dixie, and I

walked 20 miles and camped uphill from a stream that evening, on an old grassy roadbed. They pitched tents, but expecting no rain I chose to sleep under the night sky. Sometime in early morning I was awakened by the damp splash of raindrops, and mentally kicked myself. Knowing I had no time to put up my shelter without everything getting soaked anyway, I rolled my groundcloth around me and the sleeping bag, cocoon-like. I did not keep dry. When it was light enough, I stuffed everything into my pack, put on wet boots, and hiked ahead of the others. At first I had been upset with myself and disgusted with all the wet gear I had to carry. But nature would not allow the mood to go unchallenged as I strode over fields, stone fences, farm roads, and low mountains. Cool rain on the hot earth smelled musty and clean at the same time. Gray juncos continued their game of tag, as they had since Maine, feeding along the trail until I had come nearly alongside, then flitting ahead a few more feet. Of all the birds I've seen, I believe they are the ones least afraid of humans.

I picked ripe red and black raspberries found growing along fence rows and ate small undeveloped milkweed pods, (they have a mild, nutty flavor). Wildflowers grew throughout the open spaces, some fields completely enveloped by their color. Despite being wet and carrying heavy, waterlogged equipment, I thought the day a masterpiece of work.

After 10 miles we all arrived at Winturri Shelter within minutes of each other and I chose to stay and try to dry my equipment. It soon began raining again so Q-Tip and Dixie stayed also. Everything hung from the inside clothesline stayed wet, but my body heat somewhat dried the sleeping bag overnight.

The next day we all extended ourselves, trying to make up lost time and reach Pico Camp, 20.7 miles away. It was hot then, and extremely humid with a shortage of water along the way. In the afternoon, as rain threatened, we hurried along the steepening trail, gasping for air on the uphills, sweating more than I ever thought possible, but still pushed hard. At one point, near Sherburne Pass, having become dizzy, I stopped to rest. Then when my vision began breaking up like bad television reception, I knew I was probably suffering from heat exhaustion. It was a bad situation but I was heartened to know we were near Sherburne Pass with the Inn at Long Trail no more than a mile and-a-half distant. It seemed a galaxy away, though as dark clouds hovered, and I was forced to slow down behind the others.

Raindrops were just beginning to fall as I reached Highway 4 and the Inn. The others were already there and though Pico Camp was only 2.4 miles away, I announced my intentions to go no farther. By then we'd caught up to Avi and two other hikers and they also decided to stay the night, except for Q-Tip. Because Max wasn't allowed into the rooms, they went on to Pico.

After a shower and lots of liquids I felt better. The Inn is a great, rustic old place with a natural wood finish and I began to enjoy the surroundings. Sitting in the attached Irish pub, I had a meal, and later, after cleaning gear and resting, spent part of the evening with pints of Guinness, completely at ease. Murray, the bartender, owner, and desk clerk, played tapes of Irish bands over the stereo and I told him about a favorite group of mine, Seamaisin, who performed around my home town. He surprised me by saying he had their tape and knew the leader, John Kennedy, who planned to visit in the area soon, and would probably stop at the pub.

John and I became acquainted when I interviewed him for a newspaper story about the band, and we later became friends as I followed the group's progress. He didn't know about my Appalachian adventure so I left him a note with Murray as a surprise. I later learned John came by the next day so we barely missed meeting there in Vermont. While the trail seemed long and winding and expanded my senses, the event at the inn proved the world is sometimes smaller than we believe.

We stayed for breakfast at the Inn not only because it came with the room, but simply because it was there. Feeling really good after the food and rest, I nevertheless vowed to plan the rest of my trip one day at a time; to pace myself more intelligently. I hiked accordingly up Killington Mountain where the AT merged with Vermont's Long Trail for 98 miles. With the weather cooler and less humid, water was becoming harder to find. So springs were welcome sights.

A small spring near the summit of Killington ran cold and clear, and stands out in my mind as tasting better than any water I had ever drunk before.

Water, at that point, was possibly better than food when we found it. Consequently, we dipped it from places we would ordinarily not have. We found one day where a spring barely seeped from the ground, collecting in a small, muddy pool, full of debris. I still had a little water with me so passed it up. Avi though, scooped enough to fill his bottle halfway. He told me later that when he drank from the bottle he saw a small salamander swimming at the bottom, so closed his teeth to serve as a screen. He often drank what I thought was pretty evil-looking stuff but never suffered ill effects from it as far as I know.

I hiked less than 10 miles that day and 17 the next, with a 1-mile side trip into the tiny village of Clarendon. I resupplied there with enough food to get to Manchester Center, about 33 miles away. By then the others were ahead and I hiked alone, meeting northbounders along the trail and at shelters.

After Clarendon I went 20 miles on Sunday, July 30. The weather was still less humid and mostly sunny, the mountains less difficult.

I was alone at Mad Tom Shelter that night, 3,010 feet high with an open view of the western sky and other remote, hazy mountains. The shelter was unique—a cabin really—with an open front and small windows on each end. Two sliding doors with several window panes each could be pulled across to meet at the center and make an enclosure.

With water scarce along the trail and a dry spring at the shelter I couldn't cook an evening meal, dining instead on granola bars and beef jerky. Afterward, I lay atop my sleeping bag with doors open to watch the glow of evening light make silhouettes of the mountains. At that elevation in the surrounding forest, with no other lights visible, the sunset was more intense than any other I have ever seen. It was a time to be alone.

After the sun had set and the air cooled, I pulled shut the doors and slept inside my bag. I awoke later and through the windows saw so many stars they seemed clustered in the moonless sky, touching point-to-point. Their brightness startled me. Then I saw one fall with white-light tail streaking—then another. I spent the remainder of the night half awake, half asleep on that peak extending into the sky filled with stars, unable to separate dreams from reality. In my solitude the earth in darkness had become a river flowing through time and space, beyond the stars; and upon it I moved rudderless, toward a distant, shifting shore.

Entrance to the church hostel at Delaware Water Gap

Chapter Seven

"With a loss of about 20 pounds in body weight, about four pounds in pack weight, ... I felt absolutely streamlined...

After a short trail hike from Mad Tom Shelter, some road-walking and a hitched ride, I arrived at the Zion Episcopal Church in Manchester Center, Vermont early on the morning of July 31. The church members provided a large open room for hikers to sleep in, a kitchen, and nearby bathroom and shower. I picked up a package from the post office, cleaned myself and my gear, then hung out with Avi, Q-Tip, and Dixie. Several northbound hikers were also there.

I had thought the name and number given me by the girl at Rainbow Stream in Maine was for a town near Manchester Center, but the town couldn't be found on any map there, so not wanting to stray too far from the trail, I didn't call her sister and brother-in-law after all. Just knowing that I could find help there if needed had sustained me for a lot of miles, regardless.

That evening the four of us saw Apollo 13 at the local movie house and let our minds drift from daily details. We left next morning, my 54th day on the trail, 535 miles from Katahdin, where we had started, and 1,623 yet to go.

On the gradually inclined trail leading away from town we met a lone hiker heading north, called Let it Be. He had done a lot of hiking, beginning his current trip in Florida and joining the AT in Georgia. He intended going all the way to Canada, he said, after reaching Katahdin. Obviously in good shape, he said he covered 30 to 40 miles a day, and after a lot of questions we believed him. His pack was hand-made, weighing only 17 ounces he said, and he wore running shoes with the tongues removed for air circulation; but most impressive was the low weight of his gear, about 17 pounds altogether.

After leaving Let it Be we discussed ways to lighten our own loads in anticipation of the distance ahead. We then virtually raced through the forest the next few miles, propelled by possibilities. My own feet had never felt so light; I suddenly had energy to burn. A lot of that new feeling, I'm sure, had to do with slightly easier terrain. I was also probably in the best shape of the entire trip just then—long enough on the trail to have built up my body and not yet broken down by too many long, hard days.

At Story Spring Shelter that evening the four of us spread our gear, and in turn three of us went over the other persons' equipment piece by piece, pointing out what we thought were unnecessary items. We didn't agree on all the potential discards but it was a sort of reality-check and made us look at things in a new way. When we finished I had several things set aside to mail home at the first opportunity.

We stayed at Nauheim Shelter the next night after doing 17 miles. I couldn't have known it when we separated the following morning, but the next time I would see Avi would be a long way from the trail and under very different circumstances. From Nauheim I walked a couple of miles to Highway 9, then another four miles to a motel just outside Bennington, where I could stay overnight after a visit to the post office and someplace to buy new hiking boots. Q-Tip was stopping at the post office too, so we agreed to meet there at 11:00 and have lunch. He would then leave and catch up to Avi and Dixie.

I was late getting into Bennington from the motel so missed Q-Tip but finished my errands. Among items waiting at the post office was a new waist belt for my pack. The manufacturer had sent a smaller size replacement after I had called to say I'd lost so much weight the old belt could no longer be cinched snugly. It had been leaving raw rub marks on my hips and I had taken to wrapping a towel around my waist, beneath the belt, to take up the slack.

At a discount store I found lightweight boots on sale and sent home the old, heavier ones, intending to get them back when the mountains became larger in the south. I also sent home most of the items winnowed from my pack the day before, and my bivy shelter, replacing it with a lightweight tarp. With a loss of about 20 pounds in body weight, about four pounds in pack weight, and with lighter boots, I felt absolutely streamlined heading into Massachusetts.

I enjoyed my time off in the motel. Previously I had had company when laying over in town, but now with the room completely to myself I loafed and watched television. A rainstorm came through during the night, making me glad to be there, and next morning the wet grass soaked my new boots as I walked to the trail.

During the day I took time to pick red raspberries in the clearing made for a power line along the trail. Washed with raindrops they tasted extra fresh and sweet.

I came to Seth Warner Shelter early in the afternoon and decided to stay because another storm was threatening and the next shelter was 10 miles away. Before morning there would be more northbounders at Seth Warner than at any other place I came to on the northern trail. First to arrive were two young brothers from Denmark. We talked a long time before others came in and hikers continued arriving even past dark, setting up tents nearby when the lean-to was full. There must have been at least 20 of them around.

Eight of us slept in the lean-to at close quarters, including a newspaper journalist and a photographer. Of course all talk around the picnic table had been about the trail, but I was the only southbounder so we didn't relate well. I was reminded of all the miles I had yet to go and in return described for them the mountain ranges ahead in Maine and New Hampshire.

The next day proved a long one with intermittent rain throughout. Crossing into Massachusetts early in the morning I came to MA2 and detoured a mile or so to Friendly's Restaurant for a late breakfast, then made the gradual climb up Mount Greylock, highest peak in Massachusetts at 3,500 feet. At the beginning of the slope just out of North Adams I caught up to four young men on vacation from high school who said they were going to spend the weekend on Greylock—"If we can make it that far," one said.

They had scavenged supplies from wherever they could, and were overloaded with large sleeping bags and other excess equipment. They were pausing for breath when I found them, and when I looked back later, were nowhere in sight. Greylock is a long pull upward, into the clouds, but because I was a "veteran hiker" I took pride in pushing myself past periods of exhaustion and muscle pain. I could feel a marked difference between this and what I had done a month before. There now seemed to be reserves I could call on at will.

The rain had stopped when I arrived at the summit lodge but grayish water-filled clouds swirled all about the peak. For a Saturday there weren't many visitors, presumably because of the weather conditions. Like Mount Washington in the Whites, Greylock has an access road winding up the mountain to a guest lodge and other facilities.

Earth and another hiker were at the lodge when I arrived, and I had lunch with them then quickly left the mountain, wanting to make the town of Cheshire before dark. Also, as with Mount Washington, I became anxious to move away from popular facilities and onto more remote areas of the trail.

After Greylock I traversed another mountain, but at its summit, when the trail forked, lost my way. I saw no blazes and made the mistake of assuming the AT turned right, onto the path more obviously worn. By the time I found a blue blaze and knew I'd chosen wrong, I was halfway down the mountain and went on with the hope I would rejoin the AT somewhere ahead. At the bottom though, the trail went the wrong direction and I knew I was in trouble. A couple picking wild blueberries told me the trail led only to a roadway that went nowhere near the AT. The man, in effect, told me,

"You can't get there from here."

It began to rain again as I stood in the blueberry thicket feeling sorry for myself. I had developed a large blister on the bottom of my right foot and three toes on my left foot were sore with blisters under the nails, presumably as a result of the new boots which weren't working out as well as I'd hoped.

After putting on my poncho I picked a handful of blueberries, took a deep, deep breath, and studied for a minute the mountain I would climb for the second time that day. I must have gone about a mile the wrong way down—which meant another, longer mile back. With the rain and sore feet I considered the possibility I wasn't having much fun; it became a chore just to put one foot before the other and push myself up the steep trail.

After what seemed like the longest hours of my life, white blazes eventually took me directly into Cheshire, and I followed them to St. Mary Catholic Church where I reacquainted myself with the priest in charge. He was Father Time, whom I had met on the trail in Maine. Now the name made sense to me.

The hiker facility St. Mary provided was simply the floor of a small auditorium attached to the church, with a restroom; no shower, no kitchen. The town didn't offer much, but it was nice to be in out of the rain. Shivering with cold in the emptiness of the large room, I cleaned mud from my poncho and boots. A few other hikers occupied spaces on the bare floor. Most of them, I would learn, were northbound.

Earth and his friend had arrived at Cheshire before me, wondering why they hadn't seen me on the trail since I had left Greylock before them. I was embarrassed to admit my side trip to the blueberry patch, but would find similar things happened to everyone who spent a lot of time on the trail.

That evening Earth and I walked through rain to a pizza parlor several blocks away and relaxed in the glow of neon and warmth from the ovens. He talked again about leaving. Maybe in Connecticut, he said.

I left town next morning wearing boots and socks that were wet, but at least it wasn't raining. There were almost no supplies available in Cheshire so stopping at Dalton had become a necessity. It was only a little over nine miles getting there, mostly over low, undulating countryside of pastures and farm roads. However, by Dalton I was walking with a lopsided gait because of a shin splint forming in my left leg and the other problems. The town sidewalk felt much harder than the rockbound mountains I'd been on and I lost my way, having to retrace many difficult steps.

En route to a grocery store downtown I detoured to a restaurant, and starting through the front door after grounding my pack, heard shouting from the street. Turning just in time to see Q-Tip, Dixie, and Forest Hamster waving from the bed of a moving pickup truck, I heard Q-Tip shout, "We're going to.....!", but couldn't make out all he'd said. I wondered where Hamster had come from, but knew familiar faces could pop up at the most unexpected times.

By the time I finished eating and buying food supplies I thought I knew what Q-Tip had been trying to tell me. Tom Levardi is a local resident living along the AT that wanders through Dalton and his hospitality is part of trail lore. He welcomes hikers to his front porch to refill water bottles, and sometimes feeds them ice cream, so I surmised that was where the others had gone. Levardi wasn't home when I arrived but I hooked up with my friends and we left town together. We went only three miles through what was left of the day, staying at Kay Wood Lean-to. A hiker named Pondering Pilgrim and his dog, Chester, were there with two young women, Storm and Breeze.

Clarence had also come in with Eric of America and Bewildered. Clarence had been leaving cartoons in registers all along the trail and I had met him and the others farther north. Storm and Breeze, two young women who started in Maine like us, had decided to end their hike next day and head home to North Dakota and Oklahoma. Clarence, in observance of the occasion, had gone to a nearby town and stocked up on spaghetti sauce, some edible odds and ends, and two small frosted cakes that somehow made it back to the shelter intact. We pooled dried pasta that everyone carried in their packs and cooked it over stoves as Clarence heated sauce. We then gorged on spaghetti and ramen noodles with a sugary dessert called s'mores, which was a concoction of graham crackers, chocolate, and marshmallow toasted over the campfire. Sitting around the fire later talking and listening, it became an emotional leave-taking, as though part of an extended family was lost. Attachments were easily made in those days.

The next day was cool and mostly sunny on the way to Upper Goose Pond Cabin. Despite my infirmities, I enjoyed the walk through deep, quiet woods, along trails not difficult.

I caught up to Hamster where the path neared a roadway and he told me about "trail angels" who lived nearby. The place was a blueberry farm, he said, and the owners not only provided fresh water, but sometimes home-baked cookies, and you could have all the blueberries you wanted. Hamster had just been there but walked back with me to show the way. After filling my water bottles we picked plump, ripe berries for several minutes, but I never saw either the husband or wife who owned the place. Nor were there any cookies left when I arrived, but it sure was a good rest break.

Just before reaching the cabin we crossed the Massachusetts Turnpike on a pedestrian bridge. Reaching that point was another milestone of my trip, something I'd been looking forward to. Going to Cambridge in June, as we traveled the turnpike, I noticed a sign on the bridge that said "Appalachian Trail," and turned to see if there were any hikers. I saw none but knew if things went according to plan, I would be crossing there myself sometime that summer, with a pack, headed for Georgia. Now I was, and one small part of my life seemed to have come full circle. Again, I took pride in a small accomplishment.

When crossing highways like the turnpike I often heard air horn blasts from semi-trucks. At first I put it down to ordinary traffic noise but later found it was directed at me as the truckers' form of greeting. I enjoyed the recognition and suppose they must have appreciated what we were going through. Perhaps there is a nomadic kinship involved.

The cabin at Upper Goose Pond was an entirely different kind of trail shelter. A caretaker collected $3.00 per night from hikers who slept either in the bunks upstairs, on the porch, or the cabin floor. Overflows slept outside, on the grass. There were several northbounders when we arrived and Clarence, Bewildered, and Eric of America came in after dark to lay their bags on the ground. In the morning the caretaker cooked pancakes for all guests and there was no shortage of takers lined up in the small kitchen.

Dixie had gotten an urgent message from the Forest Service to call home, by way of notes left at several trailheads, so rode into town later with the caretaker when he went for supplies. I had intended to leave that day but stayed to see if Dixie would be able to continue. Then too, the day was spectacular, with warm sun above the cool, clear air. Surrounded as we were by the pine forest with the pond just down the hill, it was the sort of scenic wonderland other people paid a lot of money to get to. I borrowed the cabin's canoe, paddled out to a small, rocky island and sunbathed for an hour, then traversed the shoreline back to the dock. Later I found a fishing pole behind the cabin and tried to catch lunch. I found just one piece of live bait however, so caught only a small panfish and cooked it on the cabin's gas stove. I shared it with Hamster and we savored every scrap.

All hikers at the cabin spent most of the day exchanging food and talking about the trail: who they'd met and how other people were doing up or down the line. A young woman hiker found a large bag of falafel meal in the hiker box and treated everyone to falafel balls fried in hot grease.

I met Mission Man there, another southbounder. His story was, to me, perhaps most intriguing of all. Being deeply religious, he had simply left his home in New Hampshire, he said, to look for another church he could join further south. I had hoped to learn more of his story but circumstances didn't permit it just then.

We learned from Dixie that his grandfather had died back home in Mississippi, but since there wasn't much he could do about it at that point, he decided to keep hiking. Next morning we left with a forecast of three more days of fair weather and the Connecticut line nearby. The date was August 9, and I had been on the trail exactly two months.

I became separated from the others as usual and hiked 21 miles that day, picking the first ripe wild blackberries along the way. Damage caused by spring tornadoes was obvious with large trees uprooted and fallen in tangled disorder. The trail was impassable for several miles so a temporary detour was routed along roadways.

Next day I went 13.5 miles, not including the 3 miles into South Egremont and back. The walk into town was mostly a futile exercise. It was a typical tourist town but the convenience store didn't accept credit cards and I was almost out of cash. I spent what remained on a cold drink and sweet roll then tried the pricey sandwich shop down the street. They accepted my credit card but $3.75 for a hamburger seemed high. Nevertheless, I had dessert and ordered two large bagels to go, knowing I would be short of food until I got to Salisbury more than 18 miles away. Increased hunger pangs would remind me of the mistake I had made in not planning better at Upper Goose Pond. I could have gotten supplies there but chose rest and recreation instead.

The mountains then were not easy but a treat compared to others. There seemed more time to enjoy the walk itself. Or maybe my conditioning had just improved to the point where the mountain walks had become an automatic reaction, and not such a concentrated strain. On the evening of Thursday, August 10, I ended my journal entry with the simple line: "Up some mountains—not like Maine, though."

I got to Salisbury, Connecticut by way of Mount Everett, Race Mountain, and Bear Mountain. Atop Bear was an observation area on the rocky bald with an amazing view of the countryside. I met two men and three children there day-hiking together. The one man and his three children were from Indianapolis, about 150 miles from where I live, and visiting the man's brother and his family who lived nearby. The father admitted he hurt just from the short distance he'd gone that day and wondered how we thru-hikers did it. His comments made me feel like a veteran of the trail. The kids were very curious about my trip on the AT, and seemed awed with the adventure, the distance I'd covered, and the miles yet to go. They were particularly interested in trail names and how we acquired them, so I explained the process.

After leaving them I hiked on down the mountain and met my second young-male nude hiker. He was walking the opposite direction, holding his shorts in front of him. I suppose it was another case of chafing but didn't ask. We exchanged brief greetings and continued walking. Actually, I only assumed he was nude; I did not turn to check his backside for clothing.

In Salisbury I rejoined Q-Tip and Dixie, went to the grocery for supplies, then bought a chicken dinner and a quart of milk for lunch eaten under the shade in front of the post office. Q-Tip was talking to a tall redheaded hiker who I later learned was the legendary Ward Leonard. Leonard had hiked the trail ten times by his own account and is reputed to have the fastest time on the AT while carrying a full pack, although the time is not specific or verifiable. While such things didn't especially interest me they are part of the trail's background. Also, Ward's somewhat aberrant behavior, particularly toward females, is a matter of record and consequently his whereabouts were the subject of discussion around many campfires.

During lunch Wandering Jack and Hummer showed up and I went with them to the ice cream shop. After I had returned to the grassy tree lawn and stood eating a large chocolate cone, I heard someone shouting, "Hey, Six-Iron! Six-Iron!"

I turned to see a van pulling to the curb and several small hands waving from the back side window. It was the children I'd met on Bear Mountain and they had news that excited them. Since I'd last seen them they had all given each other trail names. In their rush to tell me what they were they all talked at once, but I finally got it out of them. I wish I could remember what the names were, but I recall thinking at the time that they had had a lot of fun with it. They were some of the nicest kids I've ever met, and I like to believe our meeting added something memorable to their trip. It certainly added to mine. They were representative in a way, of all the defining moments that formed my lasting impressions of the trail.

Chapter Eight

Salisbury CT to Fingerboard Shelter NY
August 12-August 25

"I had gotten used to being alone, but now I felt lost; and a little desperate."

From Salisbury we walked 3.5 miles over farm fields, up ridge lines and low-lying mountains with a view back to the Taconic Range we'd just crossed.

Mission Man was at the Limestone Spring Lean-to when I arrived and Dixie and Q-Tip came soon after. My left leg and both feet were hurting more by then and I was glad to end my hiking that day.

Next morning, as Dixie and Q-Tip left on the AT, I chose to go with Mission Man on a blue blaze trail into Falls Village, where we could rejoin the AT. The new trail appeared on the map to be less difficult to walk, and anyway I was looking for someplace to lay over for a few days of recuperation. As we walked I heard more of Mission Man's story, adding to what I'd learned from him at Upper Goose Pond.

The young man had lived in New Hampshire but believing there were no more unmarried "good Christian girls" in town, he left with the express purpose of finding a reformed church to join with a better selection of eligible females. He never pretended to be a thru-hiker; simply someone enjoying the scenery and traveling cheap. I enjoyed his company because he was so easy to be with. Of all people I've met he must be one of the most secure. Though highly religious in his beliefs, I never saw him attempt to impress his ideals on anyone else. He just seemed to know what he needed for himself and went in search of it.

We passed among the morning mist of lowlands in and through Falls Village. Outside town Mission Man went north in search of a church he'd learned of and I continued south. At Highway 7, I left the white-blazed trail and walked to a diner a quarter-mile north, the lure of a real breakfast and coffee too much to resist. Halfway through the meal Mission Man appeared, saying he'd checked out the church but was going to another one nearby. Later, when we said goodbye it was for the last time. I learned from other hikers that he took a bus on down to North Carolina to continue his search. I can only hope he found everything he wanted.

Leaving the diner I noticed a blue-blazed trail just behind, headed southeast up the adjoining mountain. It was becoming hot and I wasn't looking forward to tramping that hard, paved road back to the AT, so decided to chance it, hoping the two trails would join. Walking in Connecticut had become a little humdrum after the more mountainous north, and I suppose the lure of something more unexpected appealed to me now despite the small pains.

The way up the mountain became quite steep and difficult to negotiate on narrow ledges and through dense wooded areas. I knew I hadn't done my body any favors in choosing that path, but pushed on. The sky was overcast so I couldn't pinpoint the sun but was pretty sure of directions. On finally reaching the summit, I saw the trail turn northeast and knew I was in trouble again. Switching then to an old forest road leading the opposite way, I walked until it brought me to a paved road and followed it to my right. A short walk then brought me to railroad tracks leading in the direction I thought was south.

Following the railroad bed was even more painful than either the highway or mountain path. Broken rock covered the ties, wrenching my feet, and the walk became bearable only by concentrating on the beauty of my surroundings—the air seemed clean, the trees especially green. Soon the tracks began to parallel the Housatonic River, and because the current flowed with me, I knew for sure I was headed the right way. A map told me that I should sooner or later come to West Cornwall. Nearly two hours later I entered the little town of 600 population but might as well have kept walking. Like South Egremont in Massachusetts, it too offered little to the weary thru-hiker. There were no motels, only two very expensive bed and breakfasts and no diner. Ragged and tired, I sat among the well-dressed shoppers from out of town and looked a long time at the tracks leading out. Then, after finding fresh water, I took a deep breath and set out walking again.

It was another five miles to Cornwall Bridge and according to my guide book there was a motel. Again it was one step at a time, slowly plodding. Then it began to rain and soon came a thunderstorm, sweeping the cut where the tracks lay, spray dancing off the nearby river, lightning above the higher, tree-covered slopes. The poncho helped and it didn't matter that my feet got wet; the coolness eased them. It felt like an eternity though, getting to that next town. A large concrete bridge spans the river, railroad tracks, and a small road at Cornwall Bridge. It was hard climbing the steep bank to an upper roadway but that seemed to be where the few business places were. After asking directions I walked along Highway 4 to the motel, tired but relieved.

The manager was kind and tried to help, but explained that all the rooms were taken because it was Sunday. In desperation, I asked for any sort of shelter—an old shed, covered porch, anything. But he said, sorry, there was nothing. Reluctantly I reattached my pack and hit the road, wandering aimlessly back the way I'd come. I had gotten used to being alone, but now I felt lost; and a little desperate. Then the rain drizzled to a stop and as I stood looking at the sky, remembered seeing hay wagons down the slope, beneath the bridge as I'd walked into town from West Cornwall. I found four wagons there filled with fresh baled hay and with some difficulty climbed to the top of one and spread my gear; some of it had gotten damp and needed airing. I then walked to the general store, near the motel, and bought food and a newspaper.

After eating and catching up on world events I spent that evening listening to late traffic pass over the bridge above, and watched the stars that blinked through blowing clouds. The air was clean from rain and all the smells combined reminded me of farm life when I was younger.

Next morning I returned to the grocery and lounged about their picnic table with coffee and pastry until 10:00 when I hoped a room might be ready at the motel. I signed up for two nights, then with great relief unloaded my pack, removed my boots, and collapsed on the bed with no incentive but to heal.

That evening Jack, the motel owner and manager, invited me to his family's quarters for wine. He had come from India and talked about their customs and beliefs, and the difference between there and the United States. The conversation was interesting, a change of pace from thoughts only of the trail. Hearing how difficult it is for many people in his country caused me to remember how fortunate I was; to be able to walk this beautiful country purely for recreation.

Next day Jack had calls rerouted from his office to my room so I could answer his telephone while he cut the grass. Otherwise, I took care of some strange food cravings after visits to the store. There were huge meals of cornflakes with milk and sugar eaten from my blackened cooking pot, and tacos made from tortillas, sliced bologna, tomato, lettuce, and hot sauce. While not eating, I cleaned my gear, laid it out in the sun to dry, and rested my leg while watching the news on television.

My wife had talked to our family doctor and he advised me, through her, to keep the leg elevated and massage the soreness. It seemed to be working but I began to believe two days rest wouldn't be enough. Why take a chance by returning to the trail too soon, I thought, and maybe permanently damaging the leg.

Jack had offered to drive me the nine miles into Kent next morning so I could get different boots, and from there I meant to continue hiking. Instead, I called a friend in upstate New York that night, asking if he had room for me to stay a few days. I had intended taking a bus there and back but he drove down that evening, arriving at 11:00. I left a note on my door for Jack, thanking him for his help, and rode 140 miles northwest, to the foothills of the Adirondacks. If I wouldn't be hiking at least I would be in hiking country.

For the next four days I swam in the family pool as therapy for my sore leg and caught up on reading. But I soon missed the trail. Missed the routine of waking at daylight, putting on hiking clothes, eating a cold pop-tart, stuffing everything just so into the pack and filling my water bottles. Then walking always with the thought of finding more water and looking for the water supply at the last shelter of the day. If enough was available I might wash the clothes I'd worn for hiking then put up a line on which to dry them. I'd spread the groundcloth on the wooden floor of the shelter, then the sleeping bag; cook a hot meal, read entries in the register and enter details of my golf game. Finally, I'd write in my journal, then lay there with memories of the day replaying themselves in my mind, as the sun lowered beneath the trees. Life was simple, goals realistic and attainable. Each day an adventure completed.

I bought a new pack while in New York, replacing the larger one I'd started with. I had sent home so many items I could no longer balance the load properly; everything settled to the bottom and rode too low on my back. With the new smaller pack, I now resembled a day-hiker and was usually mistaken for one. I also got back the old boots from home, the ones I'd replaced at Bennington. They felt familiar and good on my feet.

That weekend was spent at a family cabin in the Adirondacks, and while there I hiked two different trails and climbed one mountain to a fire tower. The test walks convinced me the leg was ready to go again. After seven days off the trail I arrived back in Connecticut by bus on the afternoon of August 21. It was my 74th day from Katahdin. I was excited to be back but no longer felt as much a part of the trail as I once had. The rhythm seemed gone and so did the feeling of belonging to all things around me. Even with the new pack my legs were heavy, my breathing shallow. I wondered how I could possibly make up those long miles that separated me from the others I'd begun the journey with. Yet all I could do was continue south.

I stayed that night at a campsite near Ten-Mile River,

having gone just nine miles. My groundcloth and sleeping bag were placed atop soft ferns and dry leaves, and as usual, when sleeping in the open, I hung my food bag from a tree. This involved tying one end of a nylon rope to the bag and the other end around a rock. The rock then had to be thrown precisely over a tree limb about 20 feet from the ground, being just heavy enough to launch the rope, but not so weighty it couldn't be flung that high. The bag was then hoisted about 10 feet off the ground, and the other end tied to another tree nearby. The process usually took considerable time and could be frustrating, but necessary, to hopefully, keep the food safe from marauding bears.

The weather was clear, not too hot. My feet and legs were better after the rest, even if the rest of me was out of shape.

The next day I walked across hills gradually descending to farm meadows and crossed into New York State. At a highway later was a hot dog stand 150 yards to my right. After a dog and cold iced tea I crossed a field, then a railroad track with the Appalachian Trail stop. From there, on weekends, you can take a commuter train to Grand Central Station in New York City. I had no such inclination—and it wasn't a weekend anyway. Continuing, I noticed stream beds without water and springs listed in my guide book were often dry. At the Telephone Pioneers Shelter after 14 miles on the trail, I found the water source nonexistent. At that time there was about a half-pint of water left in one bottle, so I could cook no supper. Instead I ate cold cheese and candy bars, and thought of other foods. Then awoke often during the night because of the gnawing in my stomach.

A day-hiker, arriving before dark to share the shelter, said he was there to get away from the urban stress. He spent the last minutes of daylight gathering bits of trash others had left on the trail. We then had a long conversation about the rewards of hiking as he cooked a steak and potato over an open campfire. He enjoyed the advantages of short-distance hiking as I watched and listened to my stomach rumble with envy. When he learned of my shortage next morning the day-hiker shared his water supply as he'd brought plenty from town. I was relieved, not knowing when I'd come across more.

That day was a new beginning. I slowly but surely fell back into rhythm beneath the bright sun, becoming stronger by the hour and again in tune with my goals and surroundings. I hadn't expected it to happen so soon, but was gratified.

At a highway, instead of turning with blazes I couldn't find, I continued ahead, into a suburban neighborhood. I saw old, faded white blazes there on trees before they finally disappeared altogether. The trail must have gone that way at one time, but been relocated. When I came to highway NY52, I was at the right road but the wrong intersection. Directions to the Mountain Top Store were to walk left one-half mile, but I was unknowingly already to the left of the store and walked much too far before stopping for directions. At the house where I knocked, a young man invited me in, showed me on a map where we were, and pointed the way. I was out of water except for the half-cup reserve I always kept, so he gave me ice and let me fill my bottles from the kitchen faucet.

At the store I bought a large sub, ate half and stored the rest, and drank a large Gatorade. I'd had plenty of road walking and was happy to be finally back in the trees, going upgrade. I crossed more roads that day, including the Taconic State Parkway, and came to the RPH Cabin, a concrete block building converted to a bunkhouse for hikers. Two other southbounders were there, calling themselves Casper and Knucklehead. They told me they'd been hiking with Red Greene and together had been known as The Colors. Red, they said, was somewhere ahead and they were hoping to catch him soon. Were, in fact, planning to go on yet that afternoon. They seemed worn out by the trail though, and talked desultorily about getting off at Harpers Ferry.

Later that day I walked what my guide book said was one mile to the Shenandoah General Store by way of another paved road. I'm sure it was closer to a mile and-a-half. I bought pastry and a half-gallon of milk, drinking from the carton as I walked back. Casper and Knucklehead were still resting when I arrived back at the cabin and still in their bunks when I left next morning.

It was over 26 miles to the next shelter and I didn't feel

up to that distance yet, so decided on Graymoor Friary 18 miles away. The friary had closed their hostel just that year, but I'd heard they allowed hikers to camp at the ball field, beneath a pavilion. It was a long day and I was tired, but felt the distance would be a good test of my conditioning. Along the way I met two Scoutmasters with three Boy Scouts. Not surprisingly, since it was school vacation time, there had been a lot of Scouts along the trail, in groups ranging from three or four to a couple of dozen. Most, like these, were out for only a few days. There had been some tough ups and downs that day and one of the leaders had developed cramps in his legs, so was going to a nearby road so he could try hitching to the friary. I sympathized with his pain but again was proud of my own condition, despite the recent setback. I knew I was ready to do long miles again and couldn't help comparing myself to others.

The friary is a large complex and at the gift shop where I stopped for directions I found a soda vending machine. There still hadn't been enough water along the trail and I was extremely thirsty. Sadly though, I had no change and the gift shop was closing. As I stood waiting for inspiration an older couple stopped to talk. They had noticed my pack and asked if I was hiking the AT. They said their son had walked it and we fell into conversation about experiences. Fortunately, they also provided me with change and I became a happier hiker.

Red Greene was at the pavilion when I arrived so I told him of his friends whereabouts, and later the scout group arrived. Unable to get a ride, the leader with cramps had walked all the way in, but he seemed none the worse for wear.

The Brother in charge of hikers visited later, welcoming us to Graymoor. He said there were plans underway to reopen the hostel, with help from volunteers to do needed repairs. He also said it hadn't rained for 18 days in that part of New York. From what I'd seen I thought the drought had been longer.

Red and I both slept atop heavy folding tables that night, beneath the roof. Wind swept across the open field, causing me to pull deeper into my bag. It was cold for August.

My plan had been to go into Fort Montgomery the next

day for food supplies, but when I saw how far off the trail it was I instead took a chance on hunger. There was a lot of road walking that day across the long Hudson River Bridge into Bear Mountain State Park. Traffic zoomed by to and from New York City, intruding on my senses, and I felt like a pioneer thrown into the modern world. Walking rapidly, I soon left it behind.

Through the park the trail passed caged animals, picnickers, and bathing beaches, on up Bear Mountain. It was a steep climb with false trails where the blazes weren't noticeable. Because natural water sources had dried up, and piped water in the park had somehow become contaminated, I was soon in trouble. Water at the observatory on Bear Mountain was also bad, but I met a ranger there who gave me ice water from his own supply. On West Mountain the trail was again unclear so I went slow. The sun became hotter and I became drier. There was no water at either West Mountain Shelter or the Brien Shelter. At one point I could see the gray towers of New York City, about 35 miles away, and wondered what people there were drinking, but decided I would not change places with them. I fantasized instead about ice-cold orange soda.

After 21 miles a highway led me to Lake Tiorati Circle, a bathing beach facility an extra mile round trip off the trail, in search of fluids. The concession stand was closed, but there was a soda machine and pictured on the outside was a can of orange, with beads of moisture falling along its sides, exactly the way it was in my fantasy. I inserted money and heard a satisfying clunk, then held the can in my hands—it was so very cold—gazing at it longingly, imagining how good it was going to taste in my dry throat. I held it for some moments against my hot forehead. Delay was agony, but the anticipation sublime. I drank that one, slowly at first, then quickly, but had no more change so headed for the nearby Fingerboard Shelter.

The water source for the shelter was the lake I'd just come from. I didn't look forward to the extra walk back or drinking people's bath water, even after treatment, but it seemed I had little choice.

A father and his two sons, one teenaged, the other about five, were at the rundown shelter when I arrived. The father told me they lived in New York City and had come there just for a night of camping. The younger son though, had begun to miss his mother and his own bed, so they had decided to pack up and return home before dark. Since he had no further use for the things he'd brought, the father gave me all the iced tea I could drink and I filled both water bottles and my cooking pot from his fresh water supply. He also gave me two hot dogs, one quarter of a marinated chicken, some charcoal briquettes, and about three ounces of lemon-flavored gin.

With an hour of daylight remaining after they left I started the charcoal, found a grill at the shelter, placed it over the fire ring and cooked the meat. The hot dogs were eaten first and even without garnish, buns or bread, they tasted better than anything I'd eaten in a long time. And the chicken—the main entree of my feast. Afterward, I licked my fingers so long they nearly became free of trail grime. For dessert I ate a candy bar from my meager supply of food, then lay beside the warm coals in the cooling twilight as I sipped the gin and wrote in my journal.

Since the weather was ideal and the old rock lean-to infested with mice anyway, I spread my groundcloth and sleeping bag on the tall dry grass behind. Lying there beneath the night sky I felt privileged. The end to my day had become what thru-hikers call "trail magic." I'd heard of it often enough, around other campfires, but had mostly considered it just a part of trail lore. I fell asleep considering that each time I'd needed help lately, it had come in differing forms; so perhaps there was a magic involved.

Chapter Nine

Fingerboard Shelter NY to Port Clinton PA
August 26-September 7

"...we knew if the wind rose flames would be fanned into destroying a lot of the trees."

Shortly after leaving Fingerboard Shelter in New York's Bear Mountain State Park, I passed through the Lemon Squeezer, a tall, narrow hallway formed of glaciated rock that must have split when it came to rest on the ridge. I was able to leave my pack on, but it was necessary to turn sideways and wedge myself between some of the tighter places. Larger hikers would have had a more difficult time of it. Similar rock formations were found often along the trail and would fascinate me with their diverse sculpture. Sometimes huge slabs were balanced precariously and had obviously remained so for thousands of years.

I then climbed steep rocky grades into Harriman State Park. It was still very hot, the ground drier than ever. I did not see another person inside the park, and learned later that I was probably the last hiker through before it was closed temporarily because of fire danger, and the AT rerouted onto nearby roads. On the ridge, walking wasn't so hard and the views were inspiring. I rationed my small amount of water and thought of large iced drinks just to torture myself. Along the way I met a day-hiker just starting out with a good amount of water, and, after hearing my complaint, gave me a pint. Two hours later I stopped to talk to a trail maintenance worker, who was parked nearby, and he also shared his supply with me.

After 15.6 miles I arrived at Wildcat Shelter early in the afternoon. I had heard from two northbounders on the trail that a message awaited me there. It had to be from Q-Tip, Avi, or Dixie, I surmised, knowing they would have learned about my leg problem from the grapevine, and that I was back on the trail. The message, written by Q-Tip, told me they had called Kathy and Mike, whom we'd all met earlier at Pinkham Notch, New Hampshire. The couple, he said, were going on vacation but that I could call friends of theirs if I needed anything. Because I was trying to catch up I decided not to stop. Besides, I could get to a store the next day, and the pump at the shelter was working so I had enough water for the time being.

I later learned my three friends were met at a trailhead by Kathy and Mike with cold soda and water, taken to their home where they were given use of a shower and washer, fed, given places to sleep, shuttled to stores, and taken to a restaurant. They said it was a highlight of their trip.

According to register entries, bears had been seen near the shelter recently, so I watched hopefully, but none appeared.

About noon the next day I found a farm market along a highway that intersected the trail, and though they had little in the way of trail food I did buy a chocolate malt and a bottle of Gatorade. I took with me one tomato, two bananas, and two apples to eat after I'd stopped for the day, but before reaching Wawayanda Shelter had eaten everything but one of the apples.

I'd gone only 12 miles that Sunday, August 27, over gentle hills and ridgelines, but the next shelter was almost 13 miles beyond and I didn't care to go that far under the existing conditions. The availability of water was becoming the deciding factor in my daily plans. I could have camped somewhere past Wawayanda, but there was a ranger station not far from the lean-to with an outside spigot that should furnish all the water I would need.

At first I was alone at the shelter, but just before dark Manimal arrived. He had started at Katahdin about a week after me and caught up as I slowed down with injuries. Manimal had graduated that spring from Notre Dame University in my home town so we had some things in common to talk about.

A metal bear box was provided near the shelter for safe storage of food supplies overnight, but no bears showed up there either. I did find a large container of macaroni someone had left in the box and helped myself to part of that for future supplies.

I learned from trail registers that Q-Tip, Dixie, and Avi were losing time due to knee problems and time off to see relatives, so I was finally gaining a little ground on them. Debilities continued to nag us all, not just the aged and infirm.

Next day I made about 18 miles into Unionville, New York. That detour actually took me back into New York from New Jersey but the half-mile walk into town was worth it. For $5.00 I stayed at a bunkroom attached to the end of the local tavern. The shower was a makeshift stall thrown together with plywood and sitting about 75 feet away, attached to the back side of the tavern building—and the water only ran cold. The restroom facilities were inside the tavern, so available only during business hours.

As usual, whenever near a telephone, I called home to report my progress and condition. Then I stocked up on hiker supplies at the general store and filled my stomach with restaurant food.

Inside the tavern later I heard of other hikers who had come through, including Wandering Jack and Forest Hamster. Also I saw their entries in the bunkroom register and added my own about following the golf ball. That evening I was joined in the bunkroom by one of the tavern's customers who had missed his ride home. He apparently slept well, but kept me awake most of the night with his snoring, then stood out front next morning and caught a ride to work.

Had breakfast at the restaurant that day then hiked 20 miles to Gren Anderson Shelter. Stopped for a break at Pochuck Mountain Shelter along the way and met four northbounders who drifted in singly. One, The Ordainer, had six cool beers he'd packed in from a nearby store, and offered us each one. The drink was great and the conversation interesting, but I had to carry the empty bottle with me for three days until I could dispose of it.

During the day I passed through beautiful High Point State Park in somewhat cool weather and found good water there at the visitor's center. Farther on another farm market I'd looked forward to was closed for vacation, so cold Gatorade was only a daydream.

In open country the trail crossed several miles of lowland, passed a sod farm, then a wildlife preserve. While the walking was relatively easy I found it hadn't the interest of mountain hiking. I disliked any terrain that had a feeling of sameness to it because there no longer seemed the illusion of discovery waiting just ahead.

There was no water at Anderson so I had a cold-food night while alone and a little lonely. I fell into a mood that made me question the sanity of what I was doing, to think about being home and off the trail. Such periods of doubt nagged me so that I could never really decide if I was going to finish this thing or not. But as the scenery changed, I found, so too did my feelings.

Just before leaving the trees before the highway at Culvers Gap next morning, I scattered a flock of wild turkeys, the first I'd seen so far.

My money was almost gone but at a bakery on the highway I stopped for milk and a roll. My stomach rumbled at the sight of all the things I craved, and though ATM machines weren't always handy, I vowed to have more cash with me from then on.

Past the gap the trail switched often to old woods roads then up to ridgetops. On my left, beyond sharp dropoffs, were landscapes of green valleys with farms, roads, fields, ponds and distant low-altitude mountains. I caught up to Pilgrim and a section-hiker after they had stopped for the night near a spring, but continued on a few more miles.

After a 22.5-mile day I camped that night under a tree, atop the long grass on high ground. Crickets and frogs began their usual chirping-croaking sounds just after dark, and owls called from trees just below the ridge. When I awoke later the night had taken on a dreamy quality as leaves, dead from the drought and dislodged by breeze, drifted past the full moon hanging in my outdoor bedroom. By morning they half covered my sleeping bag, causing me to feel ever more connected to the earth on which I'd slept. My mood was changed again.

It was only ten miles from there to Delaware Water Gap, Pennsylvania next day. I continued up the ridgeline and crossed the bald summit of Kittatinny Mountain in bright sunlight. At mid-morning I stopped at Sunfish Pond to eat lunch sitting on large tumbled rocks lining the shore. Soon after setting out again, I met a man going the other way who asked if I smelled smoke. As he spoke I did detect a faint odor of smoke in the air. He then introduced himself as caretaker of the nearby campsite and asked me to watch for fires as I hiked down the AT. He said he would meanwhile check out a side trail. Before leaving he said another thru-hiker called Homer was staying at his camp and asked if I knew him. I hadn't heard the name before so the caretaker escorted me to the campsite and introduced us. Homer and I then walked together down the trail as the caretaker went another direction.

After about a half-hour smoke became evident and we soon saw isolated patches of it curling upward from the deep duff of the woods. Farther along the smoke became more dense and encompassed a larger area. Then we saw in three or four places where small flames had erupted from fallen timber. The air was still then but we knew if the wind rose flames would be fanned into destroying a lot of the trees. Even with water in short supply we each threw a bottle-full onto the worst of the fires, but of course, it made little difference. Then Homer surprised me by taking a cellular telephone from his pack, asking if he should call someone.

I said, "Sure," and since we knew no other number he dialed 911 and gave the alarm. We then hiked quickstep down the trail and on the way Homer explained to me that his parents had insisted he take the phone in case of emergency, and he had been embarrassed by it. He said he would have to call and tell them they were right.

An hour after discovering the fire we came to the information center for the Delaware Water Gap National Recreation Area, just across the Pennsylvania state line. They confirmed for us that the Forest Service had gotten our message.

We signed into the hostel at Presbyterian Church of the Mountain at Water Gap, and ran into Wandering Jack who had turned his ankle on the trail and was recuperating from stress fractures. Two section-hikers were also staying overnight and I barely missed Dixie, who had left the day before. Later that day Pilgrim came in, as did the section-hiker called Xacto. They'd both just managed to get around the fire we'd found as crews were preparing to fight it. Apparently, someone called the local newspaper, because a reporter and a photographer showed up at the hostel to interview Homer and me about the fire. We later learned that because of the drought—and possibly the fire—the entire state of New Jersey had been closed to hiking and camping soon after we arrived in town. Hikers were being transported by the Forest Service from the trail to Water Gap.

Traditionally, each Thursday from June 1 to September 1, the congregation of Church of the Mountain arranges a carry-in supper at the church and all hikers in residence are invited. The day I arrived was August 31, so it was the last supper of the year. I had been aware of the approaching date for some time and planned the past several days accordingly. That supper was the answer to silent prayers made while lying hungry in shelters along the trail. I surely embarrassed myself with so many trips to the food table, but I wasn't the only one, and believe the good people of Water Gap understood. They had probably seen the same reaction many times before. In any case, they treated us wonderfully.

A bakery I found at Delaware Water Gap has to be one of the best in existence. I had found an ATM machine and was able to have anything from the bakery displays, but wanted everything and was nearly unable to choose. I finally took back to the hostel a creamy, gooey concoction that I believe was called a Peach Cloud. The next day I would choose a huge blueberry turnover and ate both without the slightest guilt.

Next morning several of us walked to a restaurant and while waiting in line I became unnerved to see a color photo of Homer and me looking back from a stack of newspapers.

rd (aka Q-Tip), with Max

Avi Benjamini (aka Avi Maria)

The author, Richard Warriner (aka Dixie), and Q-Tip

Top of the world in New Hampshire

Dixie and Fred Hoilman

Chester and Pondering Pilgrim in camp near N.O.C.

The author at Katahdin, June 8, 1995

il in Georgia

*The author in Tennessee
October, 1995*

Another mountain waiting

Keith and Pat Shaw at Monson

Brian Stark (aka Clarence)

The cell phone fire alarm had made the front page of the local paper.

That day Jack, Pilgrim, Homer and I took a shuttle into Stroudsburg for food and backpacking supplies. Jack's sore ankle only allowed a stiff hobble and although he thought he could rest it enough in a couple of days to go on, it seemed doubtful.

After we returned from Stroudsburg, I spent the remainder of that day at the hostel because it was too late to get a good start on the trail. The rest felt good in any case, even though I knew Dixie was probably pulling away from me again.

Going up the wooded ridge south of Water Gap next day, I could see back across to the southern slope below Sunfish Pond where the fire had started. It was still burning and just then a plane flew over, dropping chemicals onto the smoking area. I later learned the fire burned for a week and destroyed at least 500 acres.

Pennsylvania is noted among hikers for its rough, rocky trails, and that's no exaggeration. But rocks seemed to be almost everywhere along the AT, whatever state we were in. If I encountered a stretch of soft, dry pine needles or grass covering the path anywhere, it was extremely welcome but short-lived. And tree roots, of course, were everywhere in the mountains so that we constantly watched where we stepped. One hiker noted in a register in New Hampshire that all he had seen of the trail so far was his boots.

The first day into Pennsylvania, I caught up with Manimal who hadn't stayed over in Water Gap. He was hiking with Xacto, a Marine Corps Captain on leave whom I'd seen back at the hostel. I walked with them until we reached the steep rocky slopes leading down to Wind Gap. Manimal slowed there because of trouble he was having with a new pair of boots, and I went on.

For the first four days out of Water Gap I averaged about 18 miles a day. The weather remained hot but water was more available there than in New York and New Jersey, even if, at times, I had to go a long way to find it.

On the second day I traversed a ridge rising from Lehigh Gap that had been nearly denuded of plant life by the fumes from a zinc smelting plant previously operating in the area. Skeletons of trees braced against the empty sky, as though old people had simply died where they stood, arms upraised. I hurried through, ignoring the sign that pointed to a spring somewhere off the trail.

Stayed with Santa Claus at Allentown Shelter the third night. He was a 67-year old man with a long, snow-white beard but no hair on top, hiking to Pen Mar Park in Maryland to finish his end-to-end hike started several years before. I truly enjoyed his company but he snored loud enough to shake spider webs from the ceiling of the shelter, and I was relieved that he did not plan to walk as far as Windsor Furnace the next day. Said it was too many miles for him. Yet, just at dusk, as I looked forward to a night's sleep alone at Windsor, I saw him approaching from some distance away. In the twilight his beard appeared as a separate entity, such as swamp gas floating just above the ground.

Santa Claus seemed happy to see me and I knew he'd walked farther than usual just for the company. We did have a nice evening together even while I laughed inside at the situation. For some reason his snoring wasn't nearly as intense that night though, so I did get some needed rest. He had hiked with Dixie for a few days, he said. I read in a trail register that evening that Dixie had seen two bears on the trail the day before.

I'd begun experimenting with meal preparation lately and made an important discovery at Windsor Furnace that evening: macaroni mixed with McCormick's dry pork gravy, water, and a little Tabasco sauce makes a memorable meal, as opposed to the usual dry noodle mix with cheese sauce. I still had two Snickers bars with me and just a short walk into Port Clinton in the morning, so gave myself an extra treat after the entree.

Santa Claus told me he was definitely slowing down the next day, so I started off alone onto another tangent, following what I thought was an extension of the AT, past a man-made pond and up an old roadway. When I finally found a blaze it was blue, so I retraced the last half-mile and finally found my way, scattering another flock of wild turkeys as I crossed farmland. A big tom ran between sections of wheat, ducking his head to remain hidden.

The weather hadn't changed: hot and clear, and the last couple of miles into town were a pleasant stroll along the river. Met two older men working on the trail near town. Each Wednesday, they said, was set aside as maintenance day on the AT for a retiree group they belonged to. One of them had graduated from Notre Dame so we talked football until the thought of restaurant food overwhelmed me.

The trail emerged abruptly from the woods a quarter-mile farther along and suddenly I was passing someone's back yard, then down sidewalks following blazes painted onto telephone poles. It startled me at times to know how quickly the scene could change from deepest, darkest woodland to an urban miasma of concrete and traffic. I stopped at the post office to pick up a box from home, and as I was transferring the contents to my pack, Dixie walked up. He had gotten in the day before and stayed overnight. We exchanged news and while he then looked for the trail leading out, I went a short way out of town the other direction to eat breakfast at a diner and call home.

On my way through town I spotted the pavilion in the city park where Dixie had stayed overnight. Hikers were encouraged to use the facilities, and they were so nice I was a little sorry I hadn't chosen to lay over myself. The pavilion was large, with tables and floor space to lay sleeping pads and bags. Even racks of books were provided for reading material, and plentiful water was nearby. But I really felt like walking the trail, so after breakfast, headed up the grade out of town.

I learned a rather valuable lesson that day after eating country ham at the diner. The salt-cured meat seemed to soak up all the fluids from my body and for the rest of that day I couldn't drink enough water to satisfy my thirst. An especially bad mistake when hiking through dry countryside.

After catching up to Dixie, we walked together and stopped to camp near Sand Spring because of a good water source. The spring itself was about three-quarters of a mile down the mountainside though, so we spent considerable time on water supply.

Next morning we passed where Fort Dietrich Snyder had been built as an Indian lookout during the French and

Indian War, its construction supervised by Colonel Benjamin Franklin. We probably walked some of the same trails and drank from the same springs as he.

We hiked easy to the 501 Shelter that day, through dark woods and over the many rocks, catching up to an elderly man day-hiking. We slowed to match his stride as he talked about the history of the area, and of his wife at home, suffering with cancer. He said he needed this time in the woods to find a measure of peace, and I think we both understood. Though I believe he enjoyed our company, he said we should go on without him, knowing our pace should be faster. He had told us about a cold-water pond just ahead, down from where the trail crossed a stream. Because it was early we left the trail to find it and the man rejoined us there for a time.

The pond was near an old concrete sluice gate that might once have been part of a mill race. The water was extremely cold for such a high outdoor temperature but Dixie and I stripped off our hiking shorts and bathed, then sat on the concrete wall with our feet in the water. The air at the pond was cooled by the shade of trees around it and by the water. It had become a mellow, reflective kind of afternoon; all was quiet but for a breeze dislodging leaves turned prematurely brown. Dixie pointed out how many of the leaves falling into the water resembled tiny sailboats, and it became entrancing to watch them as the sun held in the sky and time was suspended. Dried and curled into sail-like patterns, the miniature armada caught the breeze and frantically drove briefly in one direction, then another as the wind shifted. On reaching the leeward shore each was immediately replaced by another nearing the end of its own cycle, and now too, seeking refuge in movement.

Chapter Ten

501 Shelter PA to Rod Hollow Shelter VA
September 8-September 19

"I had begun to feel I could really begin to see the end at Springer Mountain..."

The 501 Shelter near Port Clinton, Pennsylvania is an enclosed one-room building with wooden bunks and a tremendous cone-shaped skylight directly over the center. A caretaker living nearby occasionally sells cold soda and ice cream to hikers. Dixie and I were the only ones there, but a former thru-hiker who lived in the area came by to see if we needed a ride anywhere. He had done the AT the year before and just wanted to help others who were attempting the trip. I assumed he came by whenever his own schedule permitted. He suggested an all-you-can-eat buffet about ten miles away and that became our immediate choice. We overate, of course, from the endless array.

After returning us to the bunkroom, the veteran hiker left after wishing us luck, and Dixie and I, unable to move much after the meal, relaxed inside. At lean-tos farther north Dixie had shared his concerns, wondering what he'd do after the end of the trail. His college major had been Wildlife Management and he had spent a lot of his life outdoors, so thought he might apply for a masters degree and find government work. But like Avi and Q-Tip, he wasn't sure, so pondered his future as he walked, and during lazier moments off the trail. I had learned some details of growing up in Mississippi, and while considerably different from a Hoosier farmboy's life, especially considering the age difference, it was interesting to hear.

The sky looked like possible rain that evening and the wind blew hickory nuts and acorns onto the skylight at intervals throughout the night. It often sounded like shotgun blasts echoing inside the bunkroom, and I awoke wide-eyed each time. The sounds were startling, but obviously not life-threatening. I was mostly just surprised to find myself in a real room on a real bed and quickly returned to sleep.

Relatively easy terrain again the next day and 15 miles to the Bleu Blaze Shelter, a privately-owned garage converted into a hostel. We had running water, electricity, and beds. Again we were the only ones there but caught up on others by reading register entries; and I added my own golf report, writing that the ball had been reported slowing down among the rocks of Pennsylvania.

It rained softly most of the night and a little in the morning, then showered heavily for about 30 minutes during the 20 mile hike to Peters Mountain Shelter. That place, by no stretch, can be described as a "lean-to." It was more like a small A-frame mountain home with built-in ladders to an upper bunk area. A homeless family once took up residence there, according to trail talk.

Next morning I left the shelter alone at 6:30 and hurried so I could meet my nephew in Duncannon. He was driving down from his home in Rochester, New York to visit and tape some video to show my wife and family back in Indiana. They hadn't seen me for over three months and reportedly wondered what kind of shape I might be in.

I was walking down the main street of Duncannon, having told Don I would be at the post office. Without knowing, he had missed the post office, but saw this white-bearded old man who he took to be just another urban transient. He then noticed the pack, and came to a sudden, shouting stop. It was an abrupt meeting, to say the least.

Don took me to a supermarket, then to a restaurant where he watched me eat and shook his head. We looked for fuel for my stove but could find none anywhere in town. Although I hadn't enough for probably more than two more meals, there were more important considerations to me. Sufficient shelter was paramount, as was my health and the avoidance of major injuries. I always felt I would get by with cold food again if the stove fuel ran out.

After the video interview at trailhead Don and I talked more about how my trip was progressing, and I heard how everyone back home was doing. Then instead of feeling even more homesickness, strangely I was anxious to continue the hike. Maybe Don's own enthusiasm for what I was doing rejuvenated me, but I had begun to wonder on the trail how others were able to deal with the sameness of their lives. I knew I'd made the right choice in being here, and perhaps that is why I was inspired to go on. Besides, Dixie was not far ahead and I could probably relate better to him at that time than to someone from the old life.

I was back on the trail at 2:00 pm, climbing up to the ridge extending like a backbone through the checkerboard Pennsylvania farm country. Along the way I passed Hawk Rock with its panoramic view of farm roads, fields, and rivers. Birders were watching with binoculars for hawks that passed through the nearby Susquehanna River valley during migratory flights. Dixie and I were to meet at the Thelma Marks Shelter just a few miles from Duncannon, but my mind was on other things, so I passed the turnoff without noticing and went another seven miles to Darlington. After I'd arrived, I realized I'd walked over 23 miles and spent time in town relaxing with my nephew, so despite missing Dixie, it had been a very productive day.

There was a young couple at Darlington Shelter when I arrived who introduced themselves as Steve and Kathy. They said they were on vacation, doing easy miles just to get away and enjoy the countryside.

The lean-to was on an open hill at only 1,170 feet elevation but a wind blew from the north, almost directly into the open front of the shelter, so we all knew it was going to be a cold night. Kathy hung a blanket as protection from the wind and began supper on the picnic table out front, but both people became frustrated in trying to get a balky stove started. I wanted to offer mine but didn't because of the fuel shortage, waiting instead to see if they could work it out. Finally though, when they asked, I gave up the stove, explaining my reluctance. They made a note of my name and future town stops, insisting they would send me a replacement canister. When the meal was ready they called me over to share the woodland feast of boiled steak and potatoes. As usual, the big meal I'd had in town had been consumed as fuel long ago, so I was very hungry again, and satisfied I had made the right decision with the stove. A meal like they furnished is worth eating cold jerky for a couple of days.

I put on all my spare clothing that night and pulled both the tarp and ground cloth around the sleeping bag to keep warm, but slept restlessly as the covering shifted, letting in drafts of frigid air. In the morning it was too cold to linger, so I packed up early, said goodbye to my new friends who remained in their bags, and was on the trail by 7:00. It was a little more than 15 miles into Boiling Springs and mostly a valley walk over pastures, past corn and soybean fields, through intermittent patches of woods, over highways, and across country roads. I got into town about noon and couldn't believe how quickly I'd covered the distance.

At Boiling Springs I ran into Energizer Rabbit and Not So Smart at the regional headquarters building of the Appalachian Trail Conference. Rabbit, a French-Canadian from Quebec, had helped Forest Hamster prepare the Bog Reports back in Maine. We talked only a short while, sure that we would meet again on the trail.

I stoked up on body fuel at a quick-mart nearby, then looked for a hostel I'd been told was a nice place to stay. But when I made a wrong turn and didn't find it immediately, decided that since the day was pleasant and I wasn't particularly tired, I'd rather go on the few miles to Alec Kennedy Shelter. It was during that walk I entered the Blue Ridge Mountains.

Rabbit and Not So Smart stopped by Kennedy for a short break then went on to the next lean-to, otherwise I was alone. My feet were sore and tired as usual, so I was glad to be stopped. I always felt that when reaching any shelter I would simply collapse for hours when I finally got the pack off, but after 10 or 15 minutes of lying flat on my back on the wooden floor, I was rejuvenated enough to do the necessary chores before bedtime. It seemed a different kind of tiredness on the trail; one quickly dispelled by rest. That may have been due largely to my improved physical condition, or maybe it was the adrenaline rush of adventure that made each morning new, with almost no memory of how tired I'd been the day before.

Spent another cold night curled in my lightweight sleeping bag. With fall weather coming, I would obviously have to make changes again in my equipment.

Pretty easy hiking again, just the interminable rocks of Pennsylvania. Sometime that day, somewhere in the forest, I passed the halfway point of my trip. Another milestone, and even though that left over a thousand miles to go on foot, I no longer felt the distance to be so remarkable. It seemed rather to be only a continuation of what I had begun, and could, if I chose, finish.

Caught up to Rabbit and N.S.S. at Pine Grove Furnace State Park where iron ore was smelted during the Revolutionary War. We walked together to a store inside the park, which was closed, but rested there, sharing a newspaper and drinking cold sodas, all acquired from outside machines.

We all stayed at Tom's Run Shelter, four miles away. There was plenty of water from both a spring and nearby stream, but the spring was clearly preferable to me because I didn't bother to treat the water from such sources. In the beginning, I used iodine tablets to purify some water and later just carried a dropper bottle of bleach. One or two drops of bleach in a quart of water seemed to treat most water-borne bacteria that can cause illness, but I know that continued use of bleach is considered a bit dangerous. Most hikers who carried filters seemed to have abandoned them somewhere before the halfway point of their trip. They proved to be excess baggage usually, because they required a lot of care and I think most hikers preferred to spend their time on more immediate details. I know I took chances on the water, and others may say it's foolhardy to do so, but I never suffered illness such as diarrhea, nor had even an upset stomach the entire trip.

When water was available we drank up to a gallon a

day and, treated or untreated, except for only the best of cold, clear mountain springs, I was getting tired of the taste. Consequently, I'd started packing flavored drink mixes, using that whenever water was plentiful, and providing a treat sometimes at the end of day. The added nutrients probably didn't hurt, either.

Next morning Rabbit said he awoke during the night and couldn't get back to sleep, so went for a walk in the dark. He flashed his light at noises he heard and besides small animals, saw reflections from eyes high above the ground. We speculated on what it might have been and I opted for bears because I still wanted to see more than that one black, furry rump disappearing into the brush near Monson, Maine.

I went ahead of the other two next day along the trail that passed within 15 miles of Gettysburg, and through Caledonia State Park where water was available from spigots. The park was closed for the year and looked deserted. It seemed while others adjusted their lives according to the seasons we hikers kept moving, hoping the seasons wouldn't overcome us.

At Quarry Gap Shelters I stopped for a break. Twin shelters there are separated by a canopied picnic table and I lay down in one of the lean-tos to rest. It finally occurred to me that high above, coiled around one of the rafters, was a large black snake watching me. Slowly then, he slithered away and I moved to the other shelter.

Along the trail I mostly only heard the noise as snakes crawled into dry leaves along the path, but occasionally saw small garter snakes. Others had seen rattlers but I never heard of them being a problem. They were always seen far enough in advance to be avoided, I had been told. One large black snake I encountered on the trail must have either felt I was no danger or he was big enough he just didn't care. I nudged him with my boot toe but he ignored me and continued poking his head down holes looking for mice or other prey, so I stepped around him.

Black snakes normally hang around anywhere they can find a meal of mice, and that's often at the shelters. Mice themselves hang around shelters because of the crumbs of food hikers leave behind. The mice weren't normally a problem; in fact, most of us had gotten used to them by then. We simply tried to leave no food uncovered or even leave it in our packs overnight. Except where bear traffic was reported to be heavy, food bags were suspended by twine from the ceiling of the lean-tos. At most shelters the twine was already in place, with flat can lids threaded onto the string through a small hole in the lid's center. A knot tied beneath kept it in place, providing a barrier to the mice. Even so, the mice proved to be adaptable and were seen at night flinging themselves like little circus acrobats, through the air and onto food bags or packs.

It wasn't unusual to see mice scurrying across the rafters or floorboards in search of edibles, and I often heard them scratching and gnawing at packs that had food in them. The only time they really bothered me was when I awoke one night to feel tiny feet scrambling across my sleeping bag. I was on my back and from inside put my hand under the mouse and flipped him over toward the hiker sleeping next to me. The mouse may have been a bit traumatized by the experience but the hiker never stirred.

I went on that day to Rocky Mountain Shelters, having walked over 19 miles. It was another twin-shelter site and a man and wife were staying in the other one. The sky looked like coming rain.

If water sources listed in our hiker's guides were obsolete or dried up, then most shelters contained some sort of written instructions as to where water could be found. At Rocky Mountain it was a very long walk down an old logging road, then onto a highway to a spring running from the hillside. Apparently the locals often stopped there to fill containers for their own use. The water was cold, and very good. It needed no treatment, I decided.

Eighteen miles the next day with a side trip into the crossroads community of South Mountain for supplies. I didn't need much, just enough to get me into Harpers Ferry. Had a breakfast of two sausage sandwiches and milk outside the store, then walked through what looked like old-growth forest; soft needles underfoot, inside a darkened cavern of huge trees. Then it became rough going at times, up and down, up and down. Rain continued to threaten most of the day. The trail passed eventually through Pen Mar Park just after entering Maryland. I had known Santa Claus was ending the last section of his AT hike there but forgot to leave a note, offering congratulations.

They say picnickers at Pen Mar often share food with thru-hikers but I saw only two or three people and none looked like they wanted to feed me. The view from the pavilion more than made up for the lack of handouts though. By then the sky had cleared to white towering clouds and sunshine. I could probably see all of Maryland from there; at least the 40 miles of it the AT passes through.

Crossed the Mason-Dixon line just before arriving at Devil's Racecourse Shelter. The lean-to was a dirty, run-down affair with no view and nothing to recommend it but the good spring water nearby. Only one other person there—a day-hiker who wanted to show how knowledgeable he was about the outdoors and the trail, but I was in no mood to pretend interest and was probably rude. I only wanted to sleep and be on my way early next morning, before he awoke.

Walked almost 20 miles next day, past the original Washington's Monument near Boonboro, Maryland. It's a conical-shaped tower of brick standing on a hilltop, erected by the citizens of Boonboro in 1827 to honor our first president before the one in D.C. was built. I love the history of that area. The battle of South Mountain was fought nearby in the Civil War and commemorative monuments reflected the Confederate point of view, unlike other such places I've visited in the north.

Crossed many roads and highways during that day and felt as though I was hiking through suburbs. The Rocky Run Shelter I stayed at was as good as the Devils Racecourse was bad. The lean-to sat on the side of a hill, surrounded by trees and quietude, with a covered wooden bridge across a springfed stream, a picnic table on a wooden platform with railing, and even a wooden swing under a slatted roof. I was alone and made a really great spaghetti supper, eating it on the picnic platform in perfect peace.

By then I had asked my wife to try dehydrating things a bit more exotic, and she sent me tomato sauce dried into sheets of a deep-red rubbery substance, and hamburger that had been parboiled to remove the grease, and then dried to a very lightweight, gray-colored substance resembling coffee grounds. Rehydrated in water, the two items were definitely sprucing up some of my evening meals.

I found a book in the shelter and since I missed reading as much as anything else on the trail, I read from it during the meal and later, until dark.

The next day, September 17, was my 101st day from Katahdin. Since leaving Delaware Water Gap I had walked 272 miles in 16 days, not counting the extra distance into and out of towns off the trail. During that period of time no part of my body hurt so I was able to truly enjoy my surroundings and the trip itself. The experience seemed to have left me with a lot of optimism.

After descending from mountain ridges the trail joined the C&O Canal towpath that extends from Washington D.C. in the east. I followed the path three miles in the other direction, along the Potomac River, to where it converged with the Shenandoah River at Harpers Ferry. The flat and open towpath is easy walking but the miles, to me, were long, simply because there were no surprises; I could see too far ahead. I think what kept me going most of all on the AT was just wanting to see what was over the next mountain, or around the next turn.

It began raining lightly as I entered town at 1:00 pm and climbed the hill to an old hotel with hiker's rates. I had pushed myself in Pennsylvania and now felt the need of real rest. I would leave two days later, I decided, after checking for mail at the post office Monday morning.

Harpers Ferry is home to the Appalachian Trail Conference, maintainers of the AT, and visiting the offices is a must for thru-hikers. They take your photo there for the yearly hiker album and others following can check your progress. Along with Avi's photo I found Little Engine's. From the registers I knew she had had physical problems in New York state and took time off, then detoured ahead, arriving at Harpers Ferry just a few days before me. I knew Dixie was behind and heard Q-Tip was planning a few days off to visit relatives nearby, so wasn't surprised that he hadn't passed through yet.

It still rained intermittently next day as I toured the historic district, walking from the hotel along streets that slid downhill to the eastern edge of town where John Brown's raid came to a tragic end. Passing a bench sitting within an indented portion of wrought-iron fence that bordered the sidewalk, I noticed something eerily familiar. Walking to the bench I found a copy of my hometown paper dated the day before. Its appearance dumbfounded me. Finding the paper anywhere along the trail was curious enough, but how had it gotten to that park bench more than 600 miles away, 24 hours after publication? The paper was rainsoaked of course, but I could tell it had never been unfolded and read. Later, while returning to the hotel, I went out of my way to take another look—just to be sure I hadn't been hallucinating from too many trail miles and too much sun. The newspaper was just as I had found it, and I left it there in the rain, one more link in a chain of remarkable events.

Among my mail at the post office next morning was a box from Kathy and Steve, whom I'd met at Darlington Shelter. A note inside said they had looked all over Eastern Pennsylvania but could find no fuel for my stove. They apologized and enclosed a $5.00 bill, an apple, orange, and several odds and ends left over from their own trip that they'd apparently included just for fun. I'd been counting on the fuel and there was none to be found locally, but at that point I simply had faith that things would work out as they must.

I also had mail from home and a letter from Rock Solid, who had thru-hiked the AT in '93. During the planning stage of my own hike I had contacted the ATC for names of hikers over the age of 50 who had done the trail so I could ask particular questions. Rock Solid had provided me with a lot of valuable information initially, and now sent notes of encouragement to post offices along the trail.

While carrying food supplies from a convenience store to my hotel room, I surprisingly ran into Forest Hamster on the sidewalk. He said he had stayed at a campsite outside town and was just then leaving the trail by walking the towpath into Washington to meet friends. Hamster seemed more nonchalant than others in his hiking and I never asked his express purpose for being there. He had never been sure just how far he would hike that year, having previously done the southern half of the trail. By arriving at Harpers Ferry he seemed to suddenly realize he had actually completed a thru-hike and decided to go home to New Hampshire. "Time to go back to work," he said.

It was hard to say goodbye; one more familiar face missing from the trail.

Most thru-hikers consider reaching Harpers Ferry to be perhaps the most significant point of their trip. Whether traveling north or south, by arriving there, they feel their trip has become a thing of achievement. Unfortunately, it's also where many leave the trail; either because of all those mountains up north, or all those miles waiting in the south. I felt neither here nor there about the matter. I simply continued to walk.

Leaving town via the white blazes, I met a woman hiker who had lost the northbound trail at the maze of highway crossings. She said her husband might be somewhere on the path ahead and asked, if I saw him, to direct him to where she was. I did.

As always I looked for the steepest slopes leading south and assumed that's where I would soon be. After almost two days of fighting town gravity it was hard finding enough energy to get myself and my equipment up there. But I missed the sound of the wild birds' songs in early morning; the clinging dew; the sound of water splashing over rocks. As usual the rhythm soon returned and I knew I had never really been away.

The Blackburn AT Center is a lodge with quarters for the caretaker, a kitchen, lounge for hikers, and a large wrap-around porch. There is a smaller building behind the lodge with built-in bunks for hikers. When I arrived at 3:00 there was little question of going on. The accommodations were much too tempting to pass up.

The caretaker, Jester, had thru-hiked the year before and since he and I were the only ones in residence, we talked trail talk. After Jester learned of my fuel shortage we bounced down rutted mountain roads in his 4-wheeler to the highway and a 30 mile roundtrip to Frederick, Maryland where I found what I needed at an outfitter's store.

Back at the cabin Jester concocted a supper of spaghetti and garlic bread, with a salad, and later, because the night was cool, gave me wood for the stove in the bunkroom. The fire was welcome. Next morning I dined on fried potatoes and bagels with cream cheese, and coffee. My journal entry for that day reads: "I'm living too good."

The following day was 17.5 miles of mountain moguls between Blackburn and Rod Hollow Shelter. A series of 17 small ascents—with following descents—kept me going constantly up and down, testing stamina and leg strength. But I enjoyed the different terrain. Then too, I reached another milestone that day by crossing into the longest state in terms of trail miles. Virginia accounts for 550 miles of trail, about one-quarter of the AT total. Veterans talk of the "Virginia Blues," where the trail may seem it has no end and discouraged hikers consider their options. But the day I began that long stretch south, along the length of the state, I felt ready to take on anything. When announcing my plans way back in February I'd pointedly said, "I don't say I'll finish the trail—I'm only saying I'll start it."

That was a built-in cop-out for sure, but by the time I entered Virginia, I felt nothing would keep me from finishing. I had begun to feel I could really begin to see the end at Springer Mountain, though the finish was still a considerable distance away.

Chapter Eleven

Rod Hollow Shelter VA to Seely-Woodworth Shelter VA
September 20-October 4

"...I stood motionless on the trail, unable to move, afraid I could go no further."

Following the Virginia/West Virginia line south, over rolling hills and through dense forest, I sampled ripe pawpaws found on the ground. Along an open field persimmons on a tree were still green and bitter. The weather was cool and very cloudy, rain threatened constantly the day of September 20. The trail passed a rock wall along US50 that was supposedly laid out by our future first president George Washington when he was a young surveyor. Sky Meadows State Park was somewhere back in the trees. Slowly, the landscape began to seem more closed in somehow, more dense again.

Arriving at Denton Shelter late in the afternoon I found it plush in terms of trail housing, with a solar heated shower, patio, and a pavilion for cooking. The shelter itself was two levels with built-in bunks and was relatively clean. After a shower I washed my hiking clothes and hung them at the pavilion to dry.

Also there were an Englishman and a young woman who said they were section-hikers. But I would have known that, I think, by their appearance. It was unlike that of thru-hikers who had a certain look in their eyes, as though thinking of more distant places. I once caught up to Avi on the trail after not seeing him for a few hours and he appeared not to recognize me. We all had times, usually during a stretch of hard days, when we fell into that sort of zone and miles passed that we could hardly remember in retrospect. We had apparently abandoned the tedium of each step by then, and focused instead on more long-range goals—perhaps the next town, a prominent peak seen from afar, or an outstanding piece of landscape we knew lay somewhere ahead.

Entered Shenandoah National Park next day after passing the National Zoo compound. The trail roughly parallels the eastern boundary of the zoo that covers thousands of acres, and a sign warns: "No Trespassing. Violators Will Be Eaten." Occasionally there were exotic animals I couldn't name, but very unlike anything I had yet seen along the AT.

An older maintenance worker clipping briers that overhung the trail expressed an interest in talking, so I lingered a while and he showed me how to recognize blackberry plants by their five-leaf clusters. But for his brief company the trail was lonely in that northern section of the park.

There were an inordinate amount of spider webs across the trail then in Virginia. At open meadows in early morning their delicate patterns glistened with an outline of dew, but among the trees the sticky webs were nearly invisible, and a nuisance, clinging to my face as I walked.

Often first out of the shelter and onto the trail when hiking with others, I broke the webs erected overnight by diligent spiders. Actually, the webs served at times as a warning: if I suddenly found them after walking a trail where none had been before, I could be fairly certain I'd left the AT and was on a side trail. Time to go back and find the main route. When meeting northbounders I could be assured the trail ahead would be clear of webs for awhile, but by late September I seldom saw hikers going the other way. Thru-hikers had either left the trail by then or were struggling through The Wilderness farther north, toward Katahdin, and for day-hikers, vacation time was over.

The park's self-registration stand was out of forms for the required Backcountry Camping Permit so I hiked without one. There didn't appear to be many people in the park anyway, and I saw no Rangers, although the trail parallels the Blue Ridge Parkway for a long way and crosses it many times.

The park consists mostly of land once privately-owned as farms, so remnants of apple orchards struggle to live among the younger pine and hardwoods. Apples were just beginning to ripen those late days of September and I managed to find some edible ones among the culls. Their crisp, sweet taste made the autumn walk just that much more enjoyable.

Arrived at Gravel Springs Hut after another 19 miles and spent the night alone. Still no rain but it was close by. A grazing doe came to within about ten feet of the shelter but I still hoped to see bears.

From trail registers I learned Clarence had hiked a whopping 50 miles in one 24-hour period ahead of me through Shenandoah Park—using a headlamp at night, I assumed. Why he did it I never understood. Perhaps it was merely for the challenge.

Six miles from Gravel Springs next day I arrived at Elkwallow Gap Wayside, a combination grill and convenience store maintained by the park service. I bought a hamburger and a few snack supplies, and called home. I then walked seven more miles through wind and cold rain to Pass Mountain Hut, finding a large amount of bear scat on the trail.

An older man section-hiking north came in soon after me and just before dark, much to my surprise, Little Engine arrived. She had become sick again, she said, between there and Harpers Ferry, and went into a town for tests, thinking she might have Giardia. While awaiting results she got back onto the trail a few miles from Pass Mountain. I supposed that a woman hiking alone has a lot of difficulties to overcome—a lack of privacy and concern for personal safety for instance—so it was good to see Little Engine. I admired her determination and wanted to see her succeed.

The night had been very cold so we were up early next morning and Little Engine and I walked together to Panorama, another wayside 1.5 miles away. I was able to get my Backcountry Permit there and bought an expensive sweatshirt in the gift shop. Warmer clothing was being sent to General Delivery at Waynesboro but I couldn't wait that long; I was freezing in Northern Virginia.

We had sausages and pancakes with blackberry syrup at the restaurant and I considered it a king's feast. The breakfast didn't set well with Little Engine however, and she lost it in the restroom. Because of that she made the decision to hitch into nearby Luray and wait there for her test results. She hoped it was something she could treat with medication and not just her body rebelling against the strain of the long walk.

My right leg had begun feeling tender the day before, and as I walked alone from Panorama, thought I detected another shin splint like the one in my left leg at Cornwall Bridge. By the time I reached the Skyland Lodge and Restaurant later in the day I'd decided the leg needed rest, just as the other one had. To take time off at that point wasn't at all what I wanted but it was becoming obviously necessary again.

Skyland Lodge was filled so I had no choice but to walk on to Rock Spring Hut 4.5 miles away. Since Skyland was on the Blue Ridge Parkway and the trail leading to Rock Spring crossed the road farther ahead, I supposed that walking the parkway might save me some strain and shorten the distance. The pavement, of course, proved a shock to my sore leg and I wished I'd stayed on the trail. Finally, I reached a side trail leading up the mountain and, I thought, back to the AT with the hut just beyond. I failed to find the white blazes though, and retreated in frustration back down the mountain, then up to the parkway again where I'd earlier seen a map painted on a large wooden sign.

During that afternoon of crisscross trail walking I met the same German couple three times in the same general area. Polite and friendly the first time they asked about my trip, and were happy to see me again the second, but seemed puzzled on the third occasion. They may have thought me an active hiker, when in truth I was simply confused. Finally locating the right trail, I found Rock Spring Hut, having walked a lot farther than necessary on a leg that badly needed some rest.

It was colder than ever that night and I was alone but for a lot of deer who encircled the lean-to, browsing throughout the night. Their noises woke me often and because I hadn't hung my food bag, used the flashlight to make sure it wasn't bears out to steal my breakfast.

At 8:00 am Sunday I left Rock Spring in the rain, hiking 3.5 miles to Big Meadows and another lodge. I signed on for two nights there at high seasonal rates and began resting. Meals were available in the main lodge and since it rained off and on, it wasn't at all a bad place to be if I wasn't able to walk.

The next day I mostly lay in my room reading, napping, or just listening to the rain. For variety I hung about the fireplace in the main lodge where they served free coffee, and looked out at the cloud-covered mountains, wishing I was there, despite the weather. I no longer felt comfortable in such surroundings, preferring instead to be outside where things were more open. My gaze, as with others I knew, was more long-distance then. Looking toward objects on the horizon instead of in an enclosed room.

At midmorning I tested the leg on a mile hike to Big Meadows Wayside getting food supplies and found Energizer Rabbit there, not having seen him since Pennsylvania. He seemed discouraged though, saying he was having foot problems. In my condition I probably didn't offer much consolation, but assumed I would find him somewhere down the trail or hear of him through trail news. That was the last time I would see him however, sitting at a table in the wayside restaurant.

My leg seemed better that night, but I was undecided about taking a chance on it. The prices of lodging and meals were piling up on my credit card though, and the late days of autumn were passing, so I finally made the decision to leave next morning and do an easy hike to the next shelter. After one last breakfast in the lodge, I left Big Meadows at 10:30 and walked eight miles in the rain to Bearfence Mountain Hut. The leg was definitely still sore, more so than I'd realized, but I could only keep walking, hoping it would improve. It stopped raining after I reached the shelter and the sun came out, so tomorrow promised to be more pleasant.

The next day was warmer and only partially cloudy. I hiked 12.6 slow miles to Hightop Hut and along the way a southbounder called Traveler caught up, then kept pace with me. I think he craved company. Those days hikers were spread far apart and another might not be seen for days. Being in better shape than I, however, and wanting to log more miles, Traveler moved on to the next shelter while I stayed at Hightop.

That evening an owl began hooting somewhere off in the trees at 4:15 pm and I was reminded of the shortening daylight hours. In Maine I'd be up and walking by 5:00 am, but now there wasn't enough light to see blazes until about 7:00. When I got into camp now, at the end of the day, I had to set up quickly to avoid stumbling around in the darkness. Planning my next day's trip by candlelight that night, I hoped for more miles. Waynesboro was 41.3 miles away, the first trail town after leaving Shenandoah Park and a traditional layover. I was fairly certain I'd need to stop there and rest.

Amid beautiful fall weather the next day I limped along sunlit mountains and ridges separating the Shenandoah Valley on my right from the Piedmont section, that on my left rolled eastward to the ocean. Farms sectioned off into earthy shades of color marked the areas between river and forest. The roads connected everything but the path on which I walked.

My supplies were low so I stopped at a small campground store just off the trail. Because they were about to close for the season, the store had little to offer but Tylenol and Spam. The Tylenol was for my leg and the Spam for my supper (I had previously refused to carry cans that, when empty, had to be flattened and carried out for disposal, but all self-made rules of the trail are subject to change dictated by appetite). Best of all though, I found an outside phone at the camp and wished my wife a happy birthday. At Harpers Ferry I'd bought a present for her at the ATC gift shop so she'd have it by the time I called. I couldn't forget her after her support and encouragement, and sending packages to all the right places. Without those things I'd never have made it so far.

After continuing, my leg would periodically worsen and I'd need to rest. At one time it seemed to spasm and I stood motionless on the trail, unable to move, afraid I could go no further. But the problem eased minutes later and then the leg felt remarkably better.

Down a long side trail past Loft Mountain I came to a locked cabin owned by the Potomac Appalachian Trail Club. They rented the cabin to day-hikers but fortunately for me it wasn't in use when I arrived, so I set up residence on the covered back porch. I ate my Spam with crackers, hung clothes to dry, then sat on a rock outcropping behind the cabin overlooking a forested valley to the west. When the sunset was nearly complete, I spread my groundcloth and sleeping bag on the picnic table under the porch roof. The stone floor wouldn't have made a good bed and the nearby ground was rocky.

A 9-point whitetail buck and several does came to keep me company that evening, grazing around the cabin. The buck would periodically work his way near me, as close as 10 feet, and I had the feeling it was a deliberate challenge; establishing his dominance in sight of the does.

Stumbled into Calf Mountain Shelter next day after 18 miles. The shin splint had either improved or the Tylenol helped. No one else showed up, not even bears, though I had seen a lot more scat along the trail. Just before finding the shelter three day-hikers thrashing through the underbrush off the trail caught my attention. Then something stung me on the right hand and I discovered the hikers had bypassed a hornet's nest they'd found along the trail. I'd blundered into it before they had time to warn me, but I thought little of it because I'd been stung twice before up north. During the night though, I woke up several times and noticed an increasing stiffness and swelling in the hand.

From Calf Mountain I walked seven miles out of Shenandoah Park next morning, over Bear Den Mountain to Rockfish Gap. The leg still bothered me and the hand, although not painful, was swollen to the point where I couldn't bend my fingers. I was more determined than ever to take time off because healing had now become a necessity. Waynesboro is one of the larger towns I would encounter along the way and provided a little of everything I needed: food, new equipment, a drug store, and a place to stay. It was another three miles from Rockfish Gap into town and I walked so I could stop at an outfitters on the way and look at sleeping bags. I intended to replace my summer-weight model for something warmer during the colder nights surely to come. But first I stopped at a restaurant for a big break-fast and ate with my left hand. The right one, so grotesquely swollen, was hidden inside my pants pocket.

At a motor court I took the last room available and set up camp, then headed immediately for the drug store. The pharmacist recommended non-prescription drugs and a course of treatment, so I went back to the room, swallowed pills, soaked my hand in hot water, and lay on the bed with my right leg propped on a chair. I felt then more like a patient than a long-distance hiker.

That afternoon, while quietly recuperating and watch-ing football on television, I got up to answer a knock at my door and was surprised to see Dixie there. He'd just gotten into town and said he'd tried to rent a room, but when told they were all taken, asked the clerk if I was by chance reg-istered. He knew I was only a little way ahead of him from my entries at the shelters. I was pleased by the company and to see Dixie again. Neither of us could stay out of res-taurants that day and I appeased a hunger for fish at one of the fast food places. At a discount store I bought new long pants in preparation for the fall days. As usual, we cleaned our boots and most other equipment and caught up on the news of others.

By the next day, Sunday, I could see improvement in the condition of my hand, and the leg too, felt better. Dixie left for the trail about 2:30 in the afternoon while I stayed another night. On Monday I was at the post office when they opened at 8:30 and mailed home my sleeping bag. At a clothing consignment shop I bought a long-sleeved rayon shirt as extra protection over a tee-shirt.

On the sidewalk after leaving the store, I heard some-one calling my trail name and saw Q-Tip waving and then Max bounding toward me. It was great seeing more famil-iar faces and incredible that I'd run into both Dixie and Q-Tip there. Neither of them knew, of course, that the other was in town.

The local fire station people had let Q-Tip sleep on the grass outside and use the indoor restroom, as they did other hikers. He introduced me to another southbounder he'd come in with, called Java. We talked for a long time, catch-ing up. I reluctantly left the two after about an hour, stopping for another breakfast on my way to the outfitters, where I bought the replacement sleeping bag and stuffed it into my pack. The pack was now about as full as I could get it—and heavier—probably 28-30 pounds, but it all became a trade-off for the warmth I would need.

From the outfitters I immediately got a ride from a young woman who said she hadn't intended to stop, but did because of some overpowering impulse. She was pleasant and I enjoyed talking to her and her young daughter. She wished me luck and I walked from where she let me off to the trailhead, losing my way momentarily. Going back the way I'd come, I finally swallowed my pride and asked directions from a road crew, then found the trail south.

Going to Wolfe Shelter the weather was nearly ideal: blue sky and cotton clouds, with just enough warmth from the sun to penetrate cool air. Hiker's weather.

Q-Tip was uncertain about when he was leaving town and didn't show up at the shelter that night. Dixie, of course, was a day ahead now. But at least I knew about where everyone was. Avi had been leaving messages for me in trail registers, wondering what happened. I'd sent him a card c/o General Delivery, Harpers Ferry, but he apparently hadn't gotten it and was moving farther ahead.

Past Cedar Cliff the next day and Three Ridges to Harpers Creek Shelter. A good 19 mile day with great views. Was alone in the lean-to contemplating the climb next day over The Priest mountain. Northbounders had been warning me about it for some time, proclaiming it a killer. The leg felt good though, and so did the rest of me, so the challenge of The Priest was something I looked forward to.

I was out of sorts the next evening, having done The Priest in drizzly, cool weather. To me the climb didn't compare to Maine and New Hampshire's peaks, but the ascent was long and tiring. I fell for the old trickery of false summits and again despaired of finding the top. Got into Seely-Woodworth Shelter about 3:30 and almost immediately crawled into my bag to keep warm, because the temperature, once I'd stopped walking, cooled me quickly. Reluctantly, I later emerged long enough to cook, hoping the weather and my mood would change.

It rained hard all night and continued into daylight. I

couldn't remember seeing so much rain anywhere along the trail before. The wind was up and I hoped it would soon move the heavy clouds away. The air was so damp everything in the shelter became a little wet. I put off even visiting the nearby spring for water until it became an absolute necessity. At about noon I hadn't yet worked up enough courage to venture into the storm when Q-Tip and Java arrived. Every time they considered going on the wind gusted and nearby trees bent at alarming angles, so they finally settled in also. While none of us were bothered much by the rain and wind itself, we were concerned about falling limbs we could hear breaking loose from the trees.

I didn't like laying around shelters during daylight, so was determined to leave next morning no matter what. But the forecast was for clearing and hot, and while the wind still blew hard we knew that could help dry the trail overnight. Java and Q-Tip had heard over their Walkmans that a hurricane hovered off the Virginia coast and we supposed we were getting its effects. We fastened our tarps partially around the shelter's opening to deter the blowing rain and retreated into our bags, watching the open show of nature's fury while hoping an uprooted tree didn't crush us during the night.

Chapter Twelve

Seeley-Wordworth Shelter VA to Atkins VA
October 5-October 22

"The alternative was to chance sliding a long way down to where the timber began."

The weather was clear, the day warm as predicted. Along Tar Jacket Ridge and Cold Mountain sunlight streamed onto open grassy balds washed by rain. We stopped on top for a lunch break at 10:00 and watched clouds pushed by wind follow the contour of valleys separating one peak from another. Later, there were a lot of ups and downs, into and out of tree line. We did more than 24 miles that day going to Punchbowl Shelter at 2,500 feet, and for the last two or three miles I thought I had passed it by. My feet were sore and my legs limp as I struggled up the last endless incline. I was tired and knew I'd sleep well but vowed to do no more such days. As usual, that plan proved short-term.

Day-hikers came by after we had arrived but seeing the lean-to was nearly full, pitched tents nearby.

On Bluff Mountain next day we passed a marker commemorating the site where young Ottie Powell was found dead in 1890 after wandering away from school. Later Dixie, who wasn't with us at the time, told us he had stopped for a break after descending the mountain and walked into the trees along the trail. When he stepped back out he turned the wrong way and inadvertently walked back up Bluff Mountain. When he saw the marker again he knew he'd been there before and couldn't help remembering the stories of Little Ottie's ghost.

They say an apparition of the little boy makes appearances at the Punchbowl Shelter, but either he never stopped by the night we were there or we slept through the visit. Perhaps his ghost wasn't at the shelter at all, but on the mountain, drawing Dixie back to keep him company.

Q-Tip, Java and I hiked eleven miles that day before hitching a ride into Big Island, four miles from the trail. The town was no more than a combination grocery/gas station, but we filled up on fried chicken and ice cream and bought enough food supplies to get to Troutville. Next to the store was a rummage sale in progress and we all bought some remnant for hiking. I found a long-sleeved cotton turtleneck and cut the neck short. It lasted me until I left the trail in November and felt good on cold mornings.

The people there were all friendly and as usual paid a lot of attention to Max. He obviously enjoyed the rest, lounging in the sun, snapping up any scraps of hiker fare thrown his way. We all continued eating ice cream until deciding it would be just too tempting to pitch tents nearby, so moved on. This was all in contrast to the way I'd felt farther north in Shenandoah Park when I needed to be on the trail. The change in attitude may have had something to do with the company.

We hitched back to trailhead and walked an easy three miles along ridge lines to Matt's Creek Shelter, crossing the James River en route.

After more than 13 miles next day that included some long climbs, we arrived atop Apple Orchard Mountain near 3:00 pm. It was a beautiful view from the bald summit, 4,224 feet high, and since the sky was clear we decided to camp there overnight. As we lay resting on the long brown grass near the trail a man in running shorts came by and asked about our hike, so we talked about the AT. While we had at first thought him to be just a local runner we soon realized he knew a lot about the trail. Then, when he introduced himself we recognized the name of David Horton. In 1991

Horton, an ultramarathon runner, set the record for fastest time on the AT, jogging its distance without a pack from end to end in a little over 52 days.

Horton asked if we'd ever met Ward Leonard, and of course we had. Q-Tip had seen him twice and I once. Surprisingly, Horton had never met Leonard and questioned us about him. Just then someone appeared nearly at our elbows, having come undetected along the trail from the south, and Q-Tip and I immediately recognized Leonard. It was as though he had appeared on mental command and we were both temporarily speechless. After introductions were finally made Horton and Leonard spent time comparing experiences. Photos were taken and addresses exchanged, then since Leonard needed a ride into town and Horton's car was parked nearby, they walked from the mountaintop together. We sort of felt we had witnessed trail history and would relate the experience to other hikers in days to come.

After eating we climbed a nearby rock formation and as daylight faded, watched the sunset build in a spectacular, orange circle completely around the mountaintop. It was the ending of a day that, for me, marked the completion of four months and over 1,400 miles on the trail.

We knew nighttime temperatures were predicted for the low thirties, but because the sky was so clear and we were so near the stars, we put on long polypro underwear and slept in the open, without tents. That was to be the first good test of my new sleeping bag.

Dew that night was the heaviest I have ever encountered; it covered us like rain. We all folded our groundcloth tarps over us to keep dry but water dripped and ran everywhere. Long-term sleep was impossible as we twisted and turned, trying to remain dry beneath our cover. At first gray light we pulled on cold, wet socks and boots, then stowed soggy equipment. Ice that had formed on uncovered packs during the night had to be slapped away.

Descending from the summit, the sun behind was just beginning to outline the mountain in a faint glow, while a full moon still hung in the sky ahead. With blazes just visible in the dim light, frost tinting the grass and ground fog enveloping my feet, the effect was surreal. I felt an intruder in a perfect picture, yet privileged to be included in the moment.

Stopped at a shelter near noon and spread my tarp and sleeping bag to dry a while but continued on to Bobblett's Gap Shelter, 21 miles from Apple Orchard Mountain. I was first to arrive and spotted Dixie as I walked down the ridgeline to the lean-to. He had holed up during the storm as we had, he said, and was taking this day off because it was his birthday.

We'd arrived at 5:30, allowing just enough time to fix supper while our equipment dried a bit in the open air. Below 2,000 feet altitude it wasn't as cold as the night before and a lot drier, although our bags were still damp when we crawled into them for the night.

It was 17 miles to Troutville and the last section took us over rolling hills where I recognized chestnuts along the trail—probably from the year before—but didn't take time to locate the tree. Weeks before I had seen a small chestnut tree in the forest designated by a marker. Existing examples are few because of blight, but weak, undersized offspring struggle to live, having sprouted from the rotting stumps of their forebears. It was a glimpse back, into an older, less despoiled America.

The trail led to Interstate 81 and ten minutes later Q-Tip, Dixie, and I had a motel for the night. Java was getting off to spend a day with his parents, who had driven up from Tennessee.

At Troutville were packages to pick up at the post office and equipment to sort and ship home as we anticipated colder weather. That evening, after a visit to the supermarket, we quietly celebrated Dixie's birthday in the room. We hadn't picked up a lot of food supplies because of a country store not far down the line, but did stuff the room with snacks.

As we prepared to leave the room next day about noon, the tv was turned on and we found a movie just beginning. We all became immediately interested so someone went to the front desk and signed on for another night. Town gravity had reasserted itself.

We crossed fields next morning, then up a long ridgeline, making altitude. Cramps, first in one calf, then the other, slowed me, but I was able to walk them off. It was a 15-plus mile day with wide, open views of Virginia from steep cliff edges along the trail. We stayed at Campbell Shelter and were visited by the Habitual Hiker, who lives nearby. He and his wife, The Umbrella Lady, had done sections of the AT many times and Habitual had walked trails in other countries. He too is something of a trail legend because of so much time on the trail and having written guidebooks for hikers.

We discussed all the news and rumors we'd been hearing about closure of the AT in the Smokies and Georgia. Hurricane Opal, that had kept us in the shelter eight days earlier, had created havoc with blowdowns of large sections along the trail. While friends and family had thought to keep us informed about news reports they'd heard, we were aware of latest developments because such news travels quickly on the AT. The consensus of opinion was that the trail would likely be reopened by the time we got that far south.

Habitual invited us to stop at his house nearby where we met the other half of his hiking team, then offered to slackpack us for the next ten miles. "Slackpacking" involves hiking with only a little water and food while someone delivers your pack to another point down the trail that same day. Walking the trail without my pack though, I felt physically unbalanced and uncomfortable; or maybe I had just been on the trail too long.

We traveled McAfee Knob with open views of the surrounding hills and found our packs waiting as promised at a general store, one mile from trailhead. We then killed time restocking and eating ice cream in the shade of the store overhang until The Home Place restaurant opened down the road.

The restaurant is located in a large renovated farm house centered on a sprawling lawn set in the rolling countryside, not far from Blacksburg. Having heard about it from other hikers, and most recently by Habitual Hiker, we were among the first to enter when they opened at 4:00 pm, appetites primed and ready. For $8.95 they set our table with large pitchers of iced tea and lemonade and—country style—brought all the fried chicken, country ham, vegetables, rolls, and cobbler we could handle. It was worth a hundred miles of rough trail to be there.

After eating we got permission from the manager of the restaurant to camp overnight at one of their gazebos on the lawn. Since they were open until 8:00 pm, we lounged about until almost dark before spreading our sleeping bags, not wanting to create too homey a spectacle. Even so, customers stopped by to admire Max and ask about our trip. Finally, we could wait no longer, and before the last diner had left, were in our bags, ready to sleep off the effects of the grand buffet. It began raining shortly after dark and we had to lay tarps around the railing to keep dry, but the gazebo served us well as a shelter.

Next day the going was tricky over slanted rocky slopes of Brushy Mountain made slick by rain. It became necessary at times to place boot edges into the cracked seams of rock and hang onto nearby scrub pines when possible. The alternative was to chance sliding a long way down to where the timber began. It was, by necessity, slow going for a while.

Along Sinking Creek Mountain there were a lot of briers that reached onto the trail and scratched uncovered arms and legs. A difficult day in all by the time we arrived at Laurel Creek Shelter. Java and Homer were there when we arrived. The two had hiked together before I'd ever met Homer above Delaware Water Gap, but became separated, as often happens on the trail. That made five of us southbounders at the shelter; the largest group I would hike with since we'd found Hamster just north of the Whites.

With early darkness and the weather predicted to be colder yet, we were soon in our sleeping bags, but lit candles to read by and to write in our journals. We all carried flashlights, of course, but candles were easier to use for long-term activities like reading, and they were cheaper than batteries.

If we ate breakfast in the mornings it was becoming normal to do so from our bags; then a swift flurry of movement getting ready for the trail and walking simply to keep warm while hoping for a sunny hillside soon ahead. Since I was from much farther north than the others I was able to withstand the cold a little better, but we all had knit caps and gloves that we wore on colder mornings until the day warmed, and often had them on at the shelters in the evening. If the night was unusually cold we wore our caps and a clean pair of socks inside our bags.

At that time of year it wasn't nearly warm enough anymore to wash off the accumulation of dirt and sweat before nighttime, so personal hygiene took an even more distant back seat and body odor could be overwhelming. During the night I might pull the sleeping bag completely over my head to keep warm breath inside, but invariably had to seek fresh air quickly.

We hiked together for 18 miles the next day to Pine Swamp Branch Shelter. The weather sunny but cool on our skin.

Walked a little over 19 miles the next day and crossed the New River just before Pearisburg. The New is said to be the second oldest river in the world. At Highway 100 we hitched in groups the two miles into town. Usually we rode in the backs of pickup trucks so Max was never a problem. In fact, being with Q-Tip was probably a plus as people were inadvertently attracted to friendly old Max.

We all stayed at the Holy Family Church Hostel that was almost ideal in layout and convenience. Located at the top of a hill at the edge of town, it was separated from the church by about a hundred yards. It had a kitchen with gas stove and microwave, shower and bath, lounge and dining area, and wooden bunks upstairs with real mattresses. A wood stove provided heat when the nights were cold. Like other hostels, this one too had a hiker's box we rummaged through. When in town, hikers often found themselves with an excess of food or other supplies, usually because of packages from home. Or perhaps it was just extra weight they found they could do without. We probably left as much as we took overall, with circumstances dictating our changing needs. At Pearisburg there seemed to be more donations than usual.

We did a lot of walking on Pearisburg's sidewalks getting to far-flung food stores, the laundromat, and restaurants, and it was very hot there in the valley. At a grocery, quite a way from the hostel, a local woman offered us a ride as we struggled with our bags in the hot sun. Hikers present an obvious appearance with their beards, shaggy hair, and that certain demeanor, so it was no surprise she took us for what we were. We appreciated her offer and back at the hostel she spent a curious few minutes inspecting the layout and asking questions about our hike.

We were joined at the hostel the second day by two older section-hikers from Kentucky, one of whom snored intolerably that night in the bunkroom. Though Q-Tip threw various things in his direction, nothing seemed to help and sleep was intermittent at best.

After two nights at Pearisburg we left the morning of October 18, and walked 16 miles to Wapiti Shelter over moderately easy terrain. I had run out of stove fuel again and could find none in Pearisburg, so cooked over a wood fire. The two men from Kentucky were there but spared us another sleepless night by staying in a tent.

Another 16 miles the next day brought us to a campsite near a road and parking area. Homer had gotten off to meet his father and would rejoin us later. The rest of us tied our four tarps together for cover and dubbed the arrangement "tarp city." The air warmed considerably at about 10:00 that evening but then turned cold before morning. Consequently, I was in and out of my sleeping bag, but slept well on the hillside, in the open air.

We spent the following day covering 21 miles of hills and valleys to Jenkins Shelter. Along the way we met Homer's dad, who had come to hike a section with his son. Both stayed with us that night, making a full house of six. It began raining just as the last of us got into the shelter and snow flurries were predicted later for higher elevations. We decided if it was still raining the next day we'd leave later and do fewer miles.

Java was then letting me cook over his stove and in return I gave him some of the good beef jerky my wife sent. After our usual pasta meals Homer presented, with dramatic flourish, a pecan pie his grandmother had baked in Georgia and sent with his father. Our appetites, which had been simply dulled by the most ordinary of meals, sat up and took notice at the sight. We should have savored it more but our stomachs reached out and took the pie from our hands, obliterating it in seconds.

After ten miles the next morning we arrived at the top of Chestnut Knob, elevation 4,600 feet. A former fire warden's cabin made of stone had been renovated as a shelter for thru-hikers on the summit. It sat in the center of the grassy bald with wind blowing interchangeable gusts of snow and sleet as we arrived. Had there been a water source nearby we probably would have stayed the night on Chestnut Knob. Watching from the window was fascination. Howling winds created a ragged sky of clouds in constant movement among the nearby mountains and valleys. The sky was changed from bright to wintry gray, and back again. Snow or sleet sometimes fell almost horizontally around the cabin in bright sunlight. It was nature most dramatic and beautiful.

After a lunch break we shouldered our packs and faced the cold sting as we walked rapidly down the grassy mountain, across other balds, and finally into the shelter of trees. At lower elevations it became naturally warmer. We walked a total of almost 19 miles that day, arriving at Knot Maul Shelter where again there was no water. Leaving our packs at the lean-to we reversed our steps a half-mile to a stream passed on the way up the slope.

Homer and his father had planned to walk less miles and stay at another shelter behind, so just Q-Tip, Dixie, Java, and I were at Knot Maul. At 2,900 feet the air was cold and I was uncomfortable even in the new bag, partly because I had stuffed some of my damp clothing in to help it dry overnight. My boots felt like frozen blocks of wood on my feet next morning.

Fourteen miles that day along some friendly trail. It was mostly ridge and valley walks taking us into Atkins, a small crossroads community. We registered at a motel for the night in order to wash clothes, buy food, and watch a baseball world series game on tv.

I had lost more than 30 pounds of body weight since Katahdin, reducing me to about 120 pounds, but felt like a tuned machine; legs strong with new muscle, my body tempered by wind and sun. However, I must eat whenever I could. If not, I might soon be consuming muscle as fuel and real problems would follow. That meant more town stops to pack more food for the trail, and continual trips to restaurants when I had the chance.

By trial and error, and talking with other hikers, my supplies then consisted mostly of breakfast bars, beef jerky, fig bars, cheese, Snickers bars, chocolate-covered nuts, trail mix, and dry spaghetti for bulking up the traditional dry noodle dinners in foil packets (that didn't include the occasional package from home with the dried hamburger and tomato sauce). Not filling, but hopefully enough nutritional bursts to get me to the next town—and finally Georgia.

Chapter Thirteen

Atkins VA to Unicoi TN
October 23-November 3

"Even if I didn't want it to end, finishing the trail was becoming a very real possibility at last."

We didn't get away from the motel at Atkins, Virginia until 11:30 after staying the night. Walking was relatively easy with the weather warm. Along a country lane I found the Settler's Museum and stopped long enough to tour an old, unlocked schoolhouse. Strange to find something like that along the way.

We came to the headquarters building of the Mount Rogers National Recreation Area near closing time, but got permission for camping on their covered concrete porch at the rear. Plentiful water was near, although restrooms were inside the closed area. We did manage to invest in the cold drink machine before they locked the doors and wished us a pleasant night. Pizza we later ordered from the outside telephone was delivered to the front gate. Ah, wilderness, with paradise so near.

The following day found us walking along switchback ridges and lower, receding mountains through a little rain. Homer had rejoined us on the trail after saying goodbye to his parents, and we camped that evening near a stream. Q-Tip and Dixie combined their tarps for a communal cover, as did Java and Homer. I converted mine into a one-man tent, my poncho covering the end that faced the wind. Thankfully, it rained only a little during the night, and we were sheltered beneath the trees. It did become very cold again, with frost forming overnight on all tarps and exposed baggage, but I kept perfectly warm and dry.

Tracking over grassy balds next day the sun warmed us, and the fall air invigorated. The series of hills leading to Mount Rogers was more open, unlike the mountains farther north. Occasional rock outcroppings extended far above, the trail ahead visible for some distance. Walking alone, I began seeing the wild ponies of Grayson Highlands State Park, through which the trail passed. By the time I'd reached the outer boundary of the park I'd counted 26 among the small herds.

Reaching the fence that ended the park, I grounded my pack on an upward slope of grass on the outer side, and lay in the sun to watch the animals graze. I particularly admired one stallion with long mane and mahogany-colored coat that glistened in the sunlight. Though I glory in their freedom I don't consider the ponies to be truly wild; they have obviously become used to human contact. Yet, they were shy and kept their distance until I took a pop-tart from my food bag and shared it at the fence. Some ponies tentatively pushed toward me, baring their teeth to take bits of the food from my hand. Others would only take it from the grass. I suppose I was looking for a personal connection; we were after all, kindred spirits, roaming the hills.

Java caught up later and we both took a blue-blazed trail over Wilburn Ridge atop the bald. While the AT circled the base of the quarter-mile long ridge the side trail went up and over the large slabs of broken rock, providing a great view of Southern Virginia from the top. It was a real workout but felt good and reminded me of long ago in Maine.

After Grayson Highlands and Wilburn Ridge we passed through Rhododendron Gap to arrive at Thomas Knob Shelter, 5,400 feet elevation. The stone building was exposed and radiated cold but kept out most of the wind. After eating, then spreading our sleeping bags, we walked to the rock ledge just behind the shelter. From there stretched an incredibly long and open view of the western hills we would climb tomorrow. The sunset, as usual, was a light show of colors—our evening entertainment. Writing in my journal there on the ledge, I noted: "I really enjoyed today."

I wandered alone next day through the varied colors of autumn that covered the hills, making contact with the others at rest stops along the way. A feeling of sadness had come over me and finally I realized, however much I missed home I was already beginning to miss the trail because each day brought the end a little closer.

We five rejoined where the Virginia Creeper Trail intersects the AT, and decided to take the detour to Damascus. Originally, we had planned to stay at a shelter 9.5 miles from town and go in the next day. But the Creeper Trail reduced the mileage and so we chose to make the run in yet that evening.

Damascus, at the very southern edge of Virginia, is considered the number one trail town of the AT. It literally straddles the trail, and for northbounders it's a celebration opportunity for having made it through the mountains of Georgia, Tennessee, and North Carolina. It's also a time of regrouping and planning for the long haul through Virginia. For southbounders it's perhaps a more subdued celebration; by having reached that point they've come over 1,700 miles and Springer Mountain, only 451.4 miles away, has indeed become a reality.

Near Mount Rogers and along the Creeper Trail, colors were more intense than north where drought had caused most leaves to fall early and die with drabness. The AT switchbacked along the hills at higher elevation, but the route we chose was different from anything yet experienced on our trip south. We trailed through a small town, along the river where people fished from the bridge; past small warm-looking houses of weathered board (I was reminded of old Currier & Ives prints), then an old railroad bed that stretched our legs as we hurried to beat the coming darkness.

At 7:00 I was the first to arrive in town, finding my way to the Methodist Church that provides a hiker's hostel on their back lot. The old house, named "The Place," has its own kitchen, dining area, and bunk rooms both upstairs and down. It can hold a lot of hikers and a lot of them come through during the season. But now the season was nearly over and only a section-hiker and Mountain Goat Skye, a fellow southbounder I hadn't met before, were there when I arrived. Skye had been leaving messages for days in trail registers, complaining about having seen no southbounders for a long time. Now, with five of us arriving, she was getting her wish and then some. After quick showers at The Place we five hoofed it to the pizza place downtown and replaced calories burned on the back trail.

The next day we bought food supplies. I found two small canisters of fuel for my stove at the local outfitter's and borrowed an awl from him to refasten a loosening pack strap back at the hostel. We lazed about that day, meeting Lone Wolf, who came in during the afternoon. He had hiked the trail in some earlier time and was part of the support team for David Horton in the Race Across America the year before. He said he had heard from Horton about our meeting on Apple Orchard Mountain.

We stopped again at the pizza place, joined by Skye, and after eating, the owner arranged for us to watch another World Series game as guests at the fire station nearby.

After a two-night stay we left with Lone Wolf keeping us company. I thought Skye might want to hike with us but she remained in town to take care of an errand and never caught up. (Somewhere south, I later learned, she left the trail and went home to Georgia). I was feeling good in body and spirit as we drifted on toward Tennessee, knowing I'd conquered the Virginia Blues. Had in fact, enjoyed Virginia very much, and was now left with just three states to go. Even if I didn't want it to end, finishing the trail was becoming a very real possibility at last.

Back in the mountains that day I found a tree growing from the top of a large, flat rock, perhaps ten feet by ten feet square. The rock was about five feet high, and the tree's roots spread completely over it, clutching like an eagle's claws. The tree stood not more than six feet high with a slender trunk, and when I shook it lightly on its tenuous perch, the roots lifted easily. It never ceased to amaze me how determined such trees were to exist where they could find even the slightest chance. I found them growing from the cracks of large boulders, and others lived long after their root base had been pulled from the ground and they'd fallen sideways.

In the north particularly, bedrock may be only a few inches down, so tree roots must spread horizontally in order to find a solid base from which to hold the trunk. Their base is then, by necessity, flat, with no tap root to provide real support, so winds may easily topple them, tearing roots from the rock they cling to. Blowdowns along the trail had such formations lifted into the air, fanned out to resemble a flat wall of dirt and roots, and if angled just right, would provide shelter from a sudden storm.

We walked eighteen miles from Damascus and at Double Springs Shelter found the lean-to had been taken over by four deer hunters. The most disconcerting aspect to me was the gutted deer hanging from a tree just in front of the shelter. I would rather have been somewhere else, but camp sites were scarce and I was too tired to look very far afield. By then Lone Wolf had taken a detour back to town and the rest of us bunked in with the hunters, who didn't complain. They must have known the lean-to was strictly for the use of hikers and it's probably just as well that nine of us were packed in there, because it turned almost intolerably cold that night.

The hunters played cards at the picnic table in front of the shelter, with a Coleman lantern for light. Fortunately, there was no alcohol involved, only a lot of cigarette smoking that permeated the shelter and clung to our sleeping bags. They kept fairly quiet through it all and turned in early enough that we were able to sleep, except when needing to turn and found a knee or elbow waiting.

We all wore patches of blaze orange on our packs, including Max, who was the size of a small deer anyway, and my knit cap was brightly colored. But none of us was willing to leave the shelter before full light next morning because of so many hunters in the area. Some had taken stands directly on the trail, making us uncomfortable. We dared not make unnecessary noise, for fear some would shoot only at a sound, yet we hurried to get away and made 22 miles that day.

It seemed like a roller coaster ride, up and down the ranges. I finally got over Iron Mountain and across Watauga

Dam, following a roadway from there back down to the wooded trail. I was leading the others and in the dim light, among the dense growth, missed the shelter. Again. I realized my error about a mile later but by then had come to the shore of Watauga Lake. The place looked so inviting I decided to camp there for the night and wait for the others to catch up next morning.

Across the lake, perhaps 500 yards away, was a park near a highway. I considered moving to there but chose the protection of pine trees on this side. The trees stopped about a hundred feet short of the water, leaving an open area to build a fire and cook my supper. Before dark I lay my groundcloth and sleeping bag among a small cluster of pines, then sat at the fire until the lake and sky both turned black.

The long branches intertwined and extended nearly to the ground, forming a sort of cavern where I was to sleep. With the deep groundcover of brown pine needles as a mattress, the spot beneath the trees matched the hay wagon in Connecticut for quality outdoor living. I heard from Java next day that the shelter had been crowded with day-hikers, so by dumb luck I had stumbled into the right place again.

The air felt like winter when I emerged from my nest next morning, and frost lay like a thin layer of snow on the grass of the park across the lake. I walked there and waited until Java, the first hiker from my group, showed up, wondering where I'd been.

A lot of ups and downs again that day, including Pond Mountain. In Laurel Fork Gorge we walked beside a river winding through dark thickets, splashing over rocks. We stopped where the falls came roaring down a rocky chute far above. A large pool at the bottom was filled with rock and surrounded by large boulders. The atmosphere was dusky and dense, and as old as time. We sat in silence awhile, absorbed in the magic of our surroundings.

We put 15 miles behind us that day and stopped at Moreland Gap Shelter. The weather had been cloudy and cool, threatening rain. It rained most of that night but by morning had slowed to an occasional drizzle. The day continued damp and overcast. We hiked only 14 miles, but over trails that seemed to wind continually upward. At Highway 19 we walked to a grocery and replenished our bodies and packs with food.

Apple House Shelter was only one-half mile from the highway and I was always leery of staying so close to human traffic. Especially then, on Halloween night. The building was of wood, made like a small, one-room schoolhouse. It had once been used to store dynamite, and later, apples. We joked about goblins, or ghosts of previous inhabitants, but were visited only by friendly mice.

Java had gone to his nearby home for the night and offered to slackpack us the next day. We stashed our packs in the trees above the trail and carried only the bare necessities, including rain gear. Although I felt unbalanced again, it had to be some relief to my trailworn body as we climbed over the Hump Mountains, a series of balds that took us through clouds most of the day and into Roan Mountain State Park. In open places, wind tore at my poncho and the mist surrounded like a wet blanket. It became a race to get below summits to the protection of treeline again. We kept warm while walking but chilled quickly when stopping for brief rests.

Java met us with a car at a parking area adjoining the trail and I rode back with him to get the packs while the others stayed. Q-Tip was to meet his grandfather there and spend the night with him, but the area was completely socked in by clouds and he worried about his grandfather driving the mountain roads.

The temperature continued dropping while Java and I made the hour and-a-half round trip. Q-Tip's grandfather had arrived safely, so they left, and Dixie and Homer, shivering in the cold because their warmer clothing was in the packs, were glad to finally see us. Since Java was staying at home again that night, only Homer, Dixie and I continued on. It was probably another four miles to Roan High Knob Shelter, over a trail grown dangerously slick with rain. We were all fairly miserable by the time we got there and the side trail was hard to find.

The shelter, highest on the AT at 6,275 feet, is an old fire warden's cabin with a loft area. The downstairs was dirty and airy so we chose the upstairs for sleeping. It took some time to find the water source, a tiny spring downhill from the cabin. We were awakened often throughout the night by a thunderstorm on the mountain that threatened to wash us from the peak. The roof leaked in several places but we positioned our sleeping bags between growing puddles.

Wet ferns covering the ground around the cabin soaked our boots and legs as we left next morning. Down reversing switchbacks we picked our way carefully over rocks and roots. On open balds we walked through and under clouds thick with moisture; it clung to us in tiny beads that sparkled when the sun showed briefly. My poncho became a cape, flapping behind as I leaned into the wind, hurrying because it was too cold not to. Between hills, in draws running north and south, we began seeing the effects of Hurricane Opal. Where one tree had fallen it caught others and created a tumbled mass with tangled roots still holding the earth, fanning into the sky. Openings had been cut through with chain saws for our benefit. Work crews, both local and those brought in from more distant places, had done an extraordinary job.

Passing over Roan High Bluff, we walked to Iron Mountain Gap and down the highway through a mile of rain to a grocery that had little to offer but tobacco. We pried reluctant conversation from the owner and drank soda until the worst of the shower had passed; then back up the slippery highway to Unaka Mountain where John Muir walked through on his way to the gulf coast in 1867. On the other side of the mountain we trailed single file through a wide, sloping meadow called Beauty Spot. By then Q-Tip and Java had rejoined us.

We stayed at Cherry Gap Shelter and left early, bound for Erwin, 16 miles away—to dry out, clean up, and rejuvenate. I had begun to feel the miles stretching and didn't know if I was wearing out or just needed a day off. The cold and damp continued as we walked quickly up and over the rises in land, then along trails turning again through rhododendrons and stands of large pine trees.

At the Nolichucky River we arranged a ride into town with a campground resident. Java went to his home in Kingsport and the rest of us dragged our wet gear into a laundromat. It felt good to be inside, especially around the warmth of the dryers. While our clothes washed, Dixie made a call to Fred and Dixie Hoilman. The couple had been hiking northbound when he met them on the trail in New Hampshire and they said to call when we reached Erwin. We didn't know what to expect, not even sure if we should eat before they picked us up.

They couldn't have been nicer, treating us like old friends at a time when we needed it most. We were taken to the lower floor of their rural home near Unicoi, to a large room with its own shower and bath, one large bed, and sleeping pads on the floor. We were invited upstairs after showers and it looked like Dixie Hoilman had been cooking all afternoon. She and her husband, having walked the trail themselves in sections, fully understood the appetites of thru-hikers. Being tired, wet, cold, and hungry, we had reached the perfect place at just the right time.

The hostel at Pearisburg, Virginia

Chapter Fourteen

Unicoi TN to South Bend IN
November 3, 1995-April 2, 1996

"...I could only sit and watch the snow fall..."

Breakfast that first morning at the Hoilmans was as spectacular as supper the night before. Afterward, I took my sleeping bag to air on their outdoor clothes line and found frost on the ground, with a touch of winter in the air; it reminded me of home in Northern Indiana. I realized then it was November 3, and I had been on the trail for almost five months.

Later we emptied our packs, cleaning and drying the equipment. We'd bought food supplies near the laundromat and sorted that into small packets, as usual. Later we walked with Fred to a pond down the road and watched him feed his stocked trout. But mostly we just lay around that day, watching Saturday football on tv, and eating. We were pampered by the accommodations.

Next morning, after another country breakfast, Fred took us to trailhead near where we had left it in the cold rain two days before. With Georgia not far away in relation to the miles covered, we all seemed to be feeling some momentum taking us into this final leg. Both singly and as a group we had all worked out tentative schedules for finishing the trail. Dixie thought sometime in December—however long it took didn't matter, he said. When he'd developed sore knees farther north that turned out to be chronic, he told us he was going to pay more attention to the scenery than the miles.

Q-Tip was more noncommittal, but thought possibly sometime in late November. I had once thought that if I pushed hard I could make it home for Thanksgiving, but getting on a plane from Atlanta that near the holiday would be unlikely, so decided to aim for November 25th, two days after Thanksgiving. Regardless of expectations, we all adhered to the old trail philosophy: "One day at a time." If completion of the AT requires "five million steps" as advertised, we knew how difficult it was to predict each step and would adjust according to conditions and our own human frailties.

Because of a trail covered with slippery, new-fallen leaves, we tried to be extra careful, but the coming season gave a sense of urgency to our walk, and we hurried as we worked our way up the mountain range from Erwin. We paused briefly at No Business Knob Shelter almost six miles away, then up and along serrated ridges until we began the descent to Spivey Gap. I was striding—probably too fast for conditions—down the sloping trail, when my right foot landed on a gnarled root hidden by leaves. My ankle turned like it had perhaps 50 times before, but this time the root was higher and the turn sharper. I heard a crack, like a dry twig breaking, and fell to the ground hoping the ankle was only sprained; refusing to admit the problem could be worse than that, but overcome by a sudden sense of finality.

Q-Tip had been close behind and found me sitting along the trail looking at my leg, hoping the pain would pass enough for me to stand. He suggested taking off my boot and massaging the ankle, and it seemed to help. But when I got the boot back on and tried walking I had to tell Q-Tip to go around, that I was only holding him up. I hobbled as best I could, but knew there was no way I would reach the next shelter before dark; if, in fact, I could continue at all.

By the time Dixie caught up minutes later realization had set in and I told him it looked like I would have to leave the trail. He walked with me to Highway 19W at Spivey Gap and offered to wait until I got a ride, but I told him to go on, that he didn't have much daylight. He crossed the road before me and disappeared into the trees on the other side as I stood, an unmoving object in the landscape, in pain, and very alone.

It was about 3:00 pm when I reached the highway and stood near a parking area trying to hitch a ride. Traffic was light that Sunday and I decided if no one stopped by 5:00 I'd have to find a spot off the road to camp. The forecast was for temperature in the 20s, but I would somehow get my tarp up and survive in my sleeping bag until morning when I'd try again for a ride to town.

At 4:55 though, a pickup stopped that had passed earlier going the other way, and the two men in the cab gave me a place on the open bed in back. They offered me a can of beer from their cooler and I accepted. Despite the cold, windy ride, the beer somehow seemed appropriate to the occasion; ruined right leg propped atop a spare tire, moving away from the trail. It was about 20 miles back to Erwin by the twisting mountain road and I considered myself fortunate to be heading for safety. I was saddened though, by how things had changed and by my sudden departure, seeing the mountains now in reverse.

After several miles we stopped temporarily while the driver, E.J., dropped his friend at home so I could ride in the warmer cab. Then along a dirt backroad E.J. pointed out where he lived, a cabin tucked into a hollow with logs painted alternately, red, white, and blue. It was built by his grandfather in the 1930s he said, and painted that way because he was patriotic. The old man had asked the colors be maintained and E.J. was honoring those wishes.

E.J. then stopped to pick up his girlfriend at her house and with Tonya driving we stopped first at the Moose Club, knowing I could call from there. Walking was painful and the trip upstairs took considerable time. E.J. talked with friends while I waited for a man obviously arguing with his girlfriend on the telephone. Twenty minutes later he was still pleading a losing case.

We finally gave up on the Moose Club and drove to E.J.'s sister's house nearby. The family had finished supper by the time we arrived but insisted on fixing me a large plate of food. Bad leg or no, my appetite was intact and I enjoyed the meal. I tried three times to reach the Hoilmans with no answer and E.J. offered his cabin as a temporary home. I had been fascinated by the place and was tempted to stay and explore the area while my leg healed from what I still hoped was a sprain, but finally thought better of it. A good decision as it turned out.

I finally reached the Hoilmans on the fourth try and arranged to meet them at the same laundromat where they'd picked us all up two days before. Back at their place they called their daughter, a nurse, who came by and looked at my leg. Her advice was to have x-rays, so Fred drove me in, and an hour later I left the hospital with a splint on my right leg, a set of crutches, and x-rays showing a double spiral fracture of the fibula, just above the ankle. Gone was the illusion I could rest a few days and play catchup behind the others. They were moving on and I was really stalled this time.

I phoned my wife to announce I was temporarily off the AT, and made reservations to fly home next day. Once again I was an overnight guest of the Hoilmans and was driven to the Tri-County Airport next morning. It would be nice to be home—but not in this way. On the flight back I was struck by the incongruity of things: five months of walking to get from Maine to Tennessee, yet in four hours I would be back in Indiana. I realized then how much I had been living every minute of each day instead of watching the world rush by in a hurry to be somewhere else.

As the plane descended toward South Bend I noticed for the first time how flat the terrain seemed. I had always thought that when I left the Appalachian Trail I would have had enough of mountains, yet here I was missing them already. I suddenly had a sense of never really being able to go home again, as though the place where I belonged was moving away as I approached; a distant light in the night sky that could be seen only by looking past it, toward something else far beyond.

————

The peace and solitude of remembrance was sanity while I healed. But immobilized by the cast on my right leg, I could only sit and watch the snow fall—and wonder how the others were doing in the south. I drifted often in spirit; lying snug in my bag at night in some shelter, with the bite of early morning cold as I hurried to be on my way, and later along the trail, walking through trees still colored by autumn; then along misty ridgelines as we descended into Georgia. My life was not confined to this house on this street. It had expanded irrevocably to be a part of something larger, something that could never be the way it had been.

In late November scenes of the trail ahead began to come less clearly to my reverie, then eventually ended. I knew it was because the trip was nearly finished for the ones I'd left, and I was no longer a part of that.

But I could begin again. And now I knew for sure what I was capable of. Knew I could rely on myself, and endure.

———————

In December, when I knew most southbounders would have finished at Springer, I wrote to several to find how their trips had concluded, and to let them know how I was doing. Little Engine said she had returned to the trail briefly after I left her in Northern Virginia, but the nagging illness returned, so she ended the hike after Shenandoah Park, and returned home to Georgia. The doctor she consulted in Virginia never discovered the cause of her problem, but she thought it might have been the physical exertion, and hoped to finish her hike by sections, or by returning for a completely new start in a couple of years.

Q-Tip said he left the group in Tennessee when he too became ill, and took a few days off to recover. He gave Max a well-deserved rest and returned to walk alone, but said it was beautiful making his way through snow in the mountains. Accompanied by family members for the last few miles, he finished his trip on December 2, and went home to Alabama.

Though I never heard back from Homer, Java, or Dixie, I learned they holed up in a Gatlinburg motel for a few days because of deep snow in the Smokies, then finished at Springer on December 1.

Manimal called when he visited South Bend to visit friends in mid-December and told me he too, had finished. We met for lunch where he showed photos of the trip, and we talked of others we'd known. He was obviously feeling a great sense of accomplishment and I was glad for him. He knew that I knew what he'd been through and believe he wanted that acknowledgment, as do all thru-hikers of the trail.

I would learn later that Wandering Jack had gotten to Harpers Ferry where his photo was taken there for the scrapbook, but could find no evidence of him farther south that year.

Clarence wrote that he had made plans to be picked up at Springer on November 18, then rest a day before a flight to Las Vegas and Thanksgiving with his family. Consequently, he planned a rigorous hiking schedule for the last two weeks, but finally, on the 16th, his body refused to move any more. He had been averaging 24 miles a day, he said, but hadn't taken into account how the increasing cold would drain his energy. That last morning he took three hours to pack up, then walked only a mile before needing to rest. Knowing his situation had become desperate, he got a ride at a roadway and ran into Avi in town. They shared a room for the night but Avi left next morning and Clarence stayed another night, suffering with diarrhea, dehydration, fever and dizziness. He called Mountain Goat Skye, who was then off the trail, and she drove Clarence to Springer. Though he feels he still has 60 miles to go on his thru-hike, Clarence says he isn't concerned about it. "Everything," he said, "is part of the overall experience."

No one I talked to had seen Energizer Rabbit past Shenandoah Park, but his name was entered into the register at the Springer Mountain Visitor's Center. Others left the trail so far back they are now hard to recall. Many, whose entries we'd read for months in the registers, did finish. Their names are many and diverse. And surely others behind made it. Our group seems to have been centrally located in the southbound pack.

Avi called in February from Connecticut and said he was moving to the west coast. His train, he said, laid over in Chicago for three hours, and would I be interested in driving over? My cast was off by then and I was again mobile, so after 1,800 miles on foot, the 90 mile drive to Chicago was trivial—and it was nice to see Avi again. His train, as it turned out, was delayed 24 hours by storms in the western plains, so I stayed over too, and we had considerable time to review trail events and talk about our impressions.

When I think about Avi, I remember one day in New Hampshire when Q-Tip, Dixie, and I caught up to him in a shelter. The day before he'd gone ahead in an apparent burst of enthusiasm and we hadn't seen him until that next afternoon. He told us he'd hiked a lot of miles the day before, much of it through rain, and had concluded with a tough climb over Big Blue Mountain. When he reached the bottom it was near dark and he was so worn out that he'd simply pitched his tent directly on the trail. In the morning he stored everything and mistakenly walked back up Big Blue. He was more than a little frustrated when he reached the top and recognized landmarks. All that work simply for the reward of getting to repeat the hardest part of it.

Avi's hike ended in November as he walked the last weeks alone. If he was to do it over, he said, he wouldn't plan it as a solo hike, preferring instead to begin with a friend. I, on the other hand, felt I'd found the best of two worlds by starting alone. I was able to hike by myself when in need of solitude and found company when I most wanted it. We agreed however, that loneliness on the trail wasn't necessarily a fatal condition. Avi described it as "bittersweet."

About half my time had been spent hiking with others, and the other half alone with my thoughts and the overpowering sense of living in the moment. Without distractions, I had found a discernible form and substance to things—texture and colors to enjoy—where, in too much of my life before, there had been only things that I could use or pass by. And I learned how important we all are to each other as social creatures. Even enjoying, briefly, the bustling crowds in small towns we found along the way.

Avi seemed restless, saying he was drawn to the western mountains, and vowed to be outdoors more. Q-Tip expressed the same general need in telephone conversations. With the trail we had all found a place we would return to in time because of the dramatic change it had brought in the quality of our lives. In retrospect we would all seem to have evolved into nearly identical lifestyle changes, or at least in the way we viewed life, and our own expectations. And while we were inescapably connected because of the shared experience, none could describe it adequately to friends or family. With other thru-hikers the understanding was obvious: we had been there, done that.

Laughing Gym wrote from North Carolina that, "In the beginning we all felt the bond that tied us together and yet set us apart from the rest of the world."

He said the trail affected him most by reinforcing a belief that, with faith, all things are possible. Others I have spoken with share his feeling while expressing it in different ways. All seem to have a sense of now being able to accomplish any goal and being able to dream a little larger. No one seemed to feel any longer a commitment to achieve the American dream in traditional terms. To have found that freedom of relying solely on oneself for survival seems to have replaced success manifested by the possession of material things. Without exception, all acknowledged a desire to never let go a quality of life found on the trail—to maintain the ties to a larger world they'd discovered along the narrow corridor of land that wandered the mountaintops from Maine to Georgia.

February, the shortest month, seemed to me the longest. It was an interim period when the old year, with its multitude of memories, drained slowly away and the new season had not yet arrived.

Then March brought on a flurry of activity as spring suddenly seemed a possibility after all. I went over my equipment again for the umpteenth time and sent my boots out to be resoled. I had decided that in April, when the weather should have moderated and most snow melted to feed the streams with good water, I would return to the mountains and continue my journey north to south. With 1,821 miles completed and just 337 to go, there was no question of my desire to finish. When I left in November we had just entered the southern section of trail that rose from the time-eroded section of Virginia, and was again becoming steeper, more closed in. I longed to be there, where the forests were turning green again, and each morning the wild birds sang. In some nearly indefinable way it seemed I was returning to a place I had finally begun to understand, and to appreciate the most. Perhaps it was just because of unfinished business, but in a way I felt like, this time, I really was going home.

The "Fontana Hilton" shelter

Chapter Fifteen

South Bend IN to Sassafras Gap NC
April 2-April 27

"...I suddenly noticed the earth before me moving. It pulsated slowly, like the rhythm of breathing."

I unbuckled the waist belt and dropped my pack, then fell along the trail, gasping for breath. This wasn't the mountains of Maine or New Hampshire but surely felt like it. My lungs and legs hurt, the upward slope gave no quarter. It was only 5.6 miles from the road at Spivey Gap to Bald Mountain Shelter in Tennessee, but it seemed like 50. Of course, it was all uphill but I felt in worse shape than the first day at Katahdin 10 months earlier.

In early April I had driven to my brother's home 75 miles west of Erwin. On April 9, he and I drove through Erwin to Spivey Gap with my hiking gear in the car trunk. But I backed off after talking to a hiker calling himself Antelope, just coming off the trail, headed north. The day was cool and overcast and he advised against starting then, saying there was a lot of snow at higher elevations. So we dropped Antelope at a motel in Erwin and then retreated west.

I had been primed and more than ready after the long wait, but good sense dictated I delay a bit longer. So I checked all my gear again, studied the trail guides and tried to plan a schedule for finishing at Springer, knowing from

experience that the schedule would be flexible by necessity. Even so, it occupied my mind and allowed me to focus
on the trail ahead.

Three days later we arrived back at Spivey. The waiting was over and I was determined to go, regardless. Fortunately, the sun was out and temperatures had risen to melt
nearly all the snow. This time Swan was just coming out of
the woods looking for a ride and said the trail wasn't bad.
She asked me to relay a message to The Bird, who was somewhere behind, and that was only the first of many messages
I would pass along for northbounders.

Preparing to leave I recalled the time five months before when I stood there in the cold for two hours on a broken ankle, hoping for a ride I was afraid would never come.
Everything looked different now from what I remembered.
I suppose how we see things depends on the situation and
our priorities, but then too, it was an entirely different time
of year. What hadn't changed was the feeling of being back
in the mountains; so much yet to see. I would be surging
against the flow of those hoping to reach Katahdin before
winter weather though, and no longer could I hope to catch
up to either Avi, Q-Tip, or Dixie. No more discussion among
us of the trail or of feelings the trail engendered. Their trip
was ended, mine renewed. I didn't know if the remainder
would be a journey of loss or discovery.

My first realization was a loss of conditioning. In December, immediately after the cast came off, I had begun
exercising in an almost frantic effort to get my right leg back
into shape. The several weeks of immobility had made me
impatient. Frustrated from long confinement, I knew I had
a lot to make up for, and each day away from the mountains
was making it harder because it was most important that I
finish; as though I had not yet become what I was capable of
being.

I hobbled up and down the walkways of a mall, first using one crutch, then just a cane. When I could walk without
support of any kind I felt as though I had reached another
mountain peak. Strangely, I found that for a brief period of
time, a slow, lopsided jog was more comfortable than walking, and I did that, too, lurching about the nearby streets. I
was finally able to leave my home in the suburbs and walked

for miles along sidewalks covered with snow and ice, into the city and back again; a single purpose to my wandering.

In concentrating on the one leg, I didn't take into account how the rest of my body had deteriorated since November. It took little time that first day on Bald Mountain however, to find how far I had fallen physically. I struggled, resting often, and began doubting again, wondering how it would be possible to go on. My lungs weren't processing enough oxygen and though my right ankle held, both legs were weak. Too weak for the mountains of the Appalachian Trail it seemed.

While taking my many rest breaks that day I was never sure if I was laying in North Carolina or Tennessee. The trail generally follows a line adjoining the two states until Fontana Dam, about 160 miles away.

Five northbounders shared the lean-to with me after I finally arrived at early evening, glad to be stopped for the day. By comparing the mileage I had yet to go with the miles they had before them, I felt mentally stronger, if not physically so.

The night was cold at the 5,516-foot level, and would be so for most of my remaining time on the trail. Patches of snow appeared in shaded pockets on some northern slopes the first couple of days, but was gradually chased by sunlight.

I detected a slight improvement in my condition on just the second day and each day thereafter. My body seemed to have memory of the way it had been the year before, and struggled to return.

It was cloudy that second day with spots of rain, and more was predicted for tomorrow. I went a few miles farther than the day before and met about 30 obviously eager northbounders on the way. Got into the shelter early enough for plenty of rest.

Sunday, April 14, became a beautiful day as the sun burned off white clouds of morning mist that clung to the hollows like something with a will to live. The sound of a waterfall came to me most gradually, a murmur at first, then increasing in volume as I found it in lowland, surrounded by the wreckage of a pioneer homestead. Enthralled by the falls and overall beauty of the surrounding hills, I missed a turn and retraced two miles of trail, most of it uphill (It had looked so different from the opposite direction). That meant I walked the same two-mile stretch three times. My senses enjoyed it but my body cried a little.

Because of the backtracking, I didn't get as far as planned and stayed at Flint Mountain Shelter. With me were two young men from Kansas, and with low food supplies and appetites in high gear they appreciated the two Snickers bars I tossed their way. I hadn't much appetite and was reminded of The Wilderness in Maine when I had eaten very little for 11 days. I thought maybe I needed another Shaw's Hiker Hostel to snap me out of it.

In the register there I continued my story of the year before about chasing the golf ball. Like any good golfer, I wrote, I had taken time off over the winter, but thought I might have gained some ground because of snow slowing the ball's progress.

Good spring water was plentiful enough for most of the southern stretch of trail and I took advantage of it, having learned about dehydration the year before.

I went a little farther the next day with one very long uphill in the morning. My lungs and legs were noticeably better but my left knee began feeling gimpy on the downhills; stomach a little queasy and still no appetite, but I decided to force a hot meal that night at the shelter.

Along the trail I passed three graves, marked with two headstones. Two North Carolina brothers, who joined the Union cause in the Civil War, along with their 15-year old cousin, were ambushed and killed by Confederates while on leave to visit family in the area.

Spent time at the Jerry Cabin Shelter, talking to Sam Waddle, a man in his 70s who was maintaining the shelter for his 23rd year. Sam told me the lean-to was constructed from a nearby stone hut used by a cattle herder long ago (I presume the herder's name was Jerry). While I ate and rested under the roof, a work crew cleared trees uprooted by hurricane winds of the year before. One large limb they cut fell on the chimney, rousing me from my stupor. I decided then I'd better get moving. It was too cold to linger anyway.

Later, after crossing Camp Creek Bald, I stopped to rest

and eat where trees and thick brush blocked the wind along a narrow ridge line. While leaning against an adjoining tree stump, I suddenly noticed the earth before me moving. It pulsated slowly, like the rhythm of breathing. Initially, I thought fatigue or strain was creating hallucination, then I discovered the motion was caused by a nearby tree. With each gust of the wind, the tree's roots, hidden just beneath the surface of the trail, strained upward, against the soil, then settled when the wind abated. I stared for some minutes, fascinated by a perception of the trail actually becoming a palpably living thing.

At Little Laurel Shelter for the night, I talked with Lazy Legs and Crazy Toes, two men from Maine hiking toward home. Like most northbounders I met, they congratulated me on being close to the end. They also asked questions about the path ahead and filled me in on what to expect going south.

It was cold at the lean-to and began raining after we were safe inside. The rain continued into darkness but I noticed later that it seemed to have stopped. In the morning I discovered why. It had turned to snow, and a dusting of it covered almost everything. Snow clung to the pines and rhododendron bushes, making the trail ahead a tunnel through white and scented green. Cold air nipped at the skin and made the blood rush. The sight and feel of my surroundings were so all-encompassing that, for a while, nothing else existed; not the past or future. Simply living the moment again was all.

I tried camping that night near the lookout tower at the summit of Rich Mountain, but strong winds threatened to relocate my tent so I moved down the trail another half-mile and made camp at lower altitude, among trees. Still the winds were strong there too, and I discovered the pup tent I'd recovered from my attic for this last section of trail had no cover for the zippered end to keep out heavy rain that threatened. I knew if it came during the night I might wake up in a wet little ball, but Hot Springs, North Carolina was only 7.5 miles away and I could make that even while lugging wet equipment.

The trail passes directly through Hot Springs, making it a necessary stop for northbound hikers who have been on the trail long enough to feel they deserve a layover. Southbounders though, are so close to the end by then they usually don't linger.

I arrived at 10:00 am and stayed the remainder of that day and overnight at the Duckett House Inn. Since I'd eaten so little on the trail I needed no food supplies, but appetite was returning so I appreciated restaurants again, and the chance to rest.

Northbounders seemed to be everywhere. They filled the church hostel space and most other available rooms. The previous year I would have been glad for all the company after time on the trail. But now I felt a stranger headed the other way, until I met Wanchor there, who had hiked part of the AT south the year before. Our paths hadn't crossed then but I remembered his trail name from register entries as he traveled several days ahead, and he remembered hearing of me.

I also looked up Dan "Wingfoot" Bruce, a resident of Hot Springs and author of The Thru-Hiker's Handbook that most of us carried to find our way. The man's been down the trail often enough to give advice in my opinion, and I enjoyed listening to everything he had to say.

Early next morning, after ascending from the valley of Hot Springs, white blazes led me along a winding country road. I stopped for a while there to sit in long grass because of the view: sun-sparkled dew still clinging to the meadows leading to mountains ahead. Birds sang nearby and I remembered the whippoorwill heard long ago in rural Indiana—but not so much anymore. Its tune, to me, was one of sweet sorrow; lonesome but hopeful somehow, crying out to others of its own kind. I guess it was just one more of the things I was searching for.

It took seven hours to walk the 14.6 miles to Roaring Forks Shelter that day. Bluff Mountain was hard but obviously I was moving better now, not stopping so often to catch my breath.

I was first into the shelter and left my gear while I went to the spring. When I returned there were two young men and one of them looked at me strangely, and said, "I thought that must be you."

He said he'd seen the golf club leaning against the lean-to, beside my pack, and remembered seeing it before. Then I recognized him, also, as the one playing the spoons with the impromptu band that performed for guests that one evening way back in Lakes of the Clouds Hut in the White Mountains the year before. He had been section-hiking then, he said, and was back to do a little more. I told him he must have found a home on the trail and he didn't argue the point.

Northbounders seemed to pass in clumps. I counted 41 of them the next day, obviously in a rush to reach Hot Springs.

More flowers were showing on hillsides as I walked to Max Patch. Too much cool wind blew across the open grassy bald for me to linger, but the view from the summit was spectacular. Billowy clouds and greening trees marked the way south. As I descended the mountain and began walking an old roadbed through woods, I saw a couple about my age approaching, and when we were close the man called out, "You must be Six-Iron." Obviously the golf club continued to work as a nametag.

I realized then who they must be. Q-Tip had called one day in February to say he'd met a man and wife near his hometown who were hiking north from Springer to attend a niece's wedding in Virginia. He asked me to look for them and also told them I would be on the trail. They called themselves, "Annie and the Salesman," and we had a great half-hour conversation there among the trees. They told me they had thru-hiked the AT in '93. We made tentative agreement to meet again at Damascus for the annual Trail Days celebration, and after I left them my spirits were buoyed.

At Groundhog Creek Shelter that night I met Slaphappy, Ladybug, and Mister Bean headed north. They seemed excited on my behalf that I was soon to finish the trail. I was already experiencing mixed feelings about that. They told me about Pondering Pilgrim and Squeaks, two other southbounders a few days ahead. I had last seen Pilgrim at Delaware Water Gap the year before and hadn't expected to see him on my restart. Pilgrim though, had always gone slow. "Going for smileage," he said, and word was that he had taken two months off during winter. I would learn much more about Squeaks in the days to come. I was anxious to

catch both hikers ahead of me. It gave more incentive suddenly to know I wasn't entirely alone in going to Georgia.

Got an early start the following day, up and over Snow-
bird Mountain. It was a long, 4 mile descent from the top
down to Highway I-40. Chipmunks darted from tree to tree
and later, after finding morel mushrooms growing on a lower
hillside, I decided I had finally walked into spring. For me
all seasons of the trail had finally come full circle.

My brother and his wife met me with food and drink
where the trail crossed the highway on its way into the Great
Smoky Mountains National Park, and soon after leaving them
I reached the Davenport Gap Shelter. A thunderstorm began minutes after I arrived, and though I wanted to go on,
the cold rain kept me inside. It quit at 5:00 but there wasn't
enough daylight left to reach the next shelter, so I stayed
the night with a section-hiker from Louisiana for company.
He said since he too was headed south he would probably
see me again. I didn't think so, because I had begun to
reclaim my long-distance stride.

From Davenport Gap it's a long, graduated climb along
switchbacks to the spine of the Smoky Mountains that joins
the peaks at an altitude of between 5,000 and 6,000 feet
generally. The day remained cloudy but rain never came.

The floor of Tri-Corner Knob Shelter was muddy and
the night air cold, but the view, though obscured by clouds,
gave a sense of being atop the world, on my own island.

I walked 15 miles the next day, April 22, matching the
distance I'd gone the day before. I felt then as good as I
ever had on the long walk, and reveled in the sense that I'd
never really left the trail. Faces had changed and the landscape was new, yet one constant remained: everything I was,
my world, consisted of what I carried with me, and the distance I had traveled at the end of day.

Shortly before noon I took a half-mile side trail to Peck's
Corner Shelter. Ordinarily, I wouldn't detour that far unless
badly in need of shelter for the night, but something drew
me, and it was there I met Red Wolf. He seemed as mystical
to me as the mountains themselves. Long hair tied behind
a weathered face, he fed the fireplace damp wood and offered me hot water. His persona, an entity of another time
and place, fit the wilderness setting.

He was a middle-aged man from the deep south who said he'd been coming there for 15 years. Since his landscape design work is finished in early spring, he explained, he spends several weeks each year exploring the park and studying plant life, then uses the findings in his business. Red Wolf carried a 70 pound pack and explored mostly side trails, seeing things most visitors to the park never do.

I learned a bit that day about plants and wildlife, and he told me he'd adopted the name of an animal he'd seen along a stream one morning. I envied his lifestyle of being able to merge his business with a natural love of the outdoors. He seemed at home there.

I walked then through a day that had cleared and become warmer. Made a side trip up Charlie's Bunion, not far off the trail and gained another perspective on the Smokies, with a wide open view from a rocky tor.

At 4:00 I again met my brother, this time at the Newfound Gap parking lot, and spent two nights at his house. I washed clothes, showered, bought food, and located more fuel for my stove. At a hiking store in Gatlinburg, I found snapshots of those friends who had passed through in late November. Thru-hikers stopping by the store are asked to pose for the bulletin board. Their faces looking back seemed of another era.

Wednesday was almost painfully beautiful. I walked above 5,000 feet through crystal clear air, and frost formed on pine needles overnight sparkled in sunlight before shattering to cover the ground like shards of opaque, white plastic. Melting in my mouth, they tasted incredibly clean. I wanted initially to only stay, unmoving as the trees, but anxious then to see everything before me.

Clingman's Dome was crossed that day. At 6,643 feet, it is the highest point on the AT, but was reached in a more gradual way, not like Katahdin in Maine. Visitors crowded the observation tower and at that height the wind was very cool. From there I could see to Siler's Bald where the trail led next.

Over Thunderhead Mountain next day, and Rocky Top, Little Bald, and some minor knobs—tree-covered hills that had no pretension to be mountains at all. Saw no bears in the park as I had hoped, but smelled their distinctive odor that day. I looked carefully but could not find the source.

The days became fairly warm, though windy, and the nights continued cold. At shelters sleeping hikers stirred often, burrowing deeper into their bags as the temperature bottomed out late at night.

Rain fell heavily the night of the 25th and lightly in the morning, but stopped 15 minutes after I left Russell Field Shelter. The day then became pleasant, walking over Shuckstack Mountain to Fontana Dam, southern boundary of the Smokies. I was glad I hadn't had to come up that slope from the other direction for its descent was steep, long, and grinding. Hikers coming from the other direction appeared dazed. I knew however, I would inevitably have to make up for it somewhere on the other side.

I intended to pause briefly at the Fontana Hilton, a donated shelter near the dam, but once there I couldn't resist staying. The Hilton is unique. Constructed on a rise overlooking Fontana Lake, it is built of stripped logs with wood plank floors. An open center area runs lengthwise, with two levels for sleeping on either side. It was remarkably clean compared to those shelters in the park.

Only minutes after leaving the Hilton next morning I noticed the strong odor of another bear, but still didn't see the animal. In Shenandoah Park, the year before, a hiker noted in a register that one had dropped from a tree five feet behind him one day as he walked. He said they both made good time then—in opposite directions. Others, it seemed, could find bears without trying, but, except for that blur in Maine, I couldn't spot one even with great effort.

It was rough going that day. Getting to Stecoah Gap was an unbelievably long and steep climb down, with, of course, a long uphill on the other side. But I found I had come a long way since Spivey Gap. Not so much in miles as in conditioning. No matter how hard it got, I was able again to find in myself the reserve to get to the top.

I meant to camp on Cheoah Bald but the only available flat, open space was occupied by others, so I descended to Sassafras Gap Shelter, arriving at 6:00 pm. It was later than usual for getting into a shelter, but I had walked 22.5 miles over terrain some considered to be nearly as difficult as Maine. I was tired, but going that far meant I could make the Nantahala Outdoor Center early the next day.

Some time was spent that night showing two young men in the shelter how I managed to travel so light. That possibility seemed to encourage some of the northbounders. Still others said they were inspired just by knowing I had made it so far.

Pilgrim, I learned, was only one day ahead then. And according to the register, Squeaks wasn't far off. It looked like I might have southbound company after all.

The leaky observation tower on Wayah Bald

Chapter Sixteen

Sassafras Gap to Springer Mountain GA
April 28-May 7

"...this next to last day would be a microcosm of all the magic I'd found along the way..."

It was only seven miles to the Nantahala Outdoor Center from Sassafras Shelter where I left early the morning of April 28. After less than an hour I caught up to Pilgrim, sleeping in his tent on a ridge along the trail. First I found his dog, Chester (The Wonder Underdog), or maybe Chester found me. He is a golden retriever, like Max, and guards his master diligently. I heard his warning bark, then recognized him, and he either detected a familiar scent or decided I was harmless. In any case, he led me to Pilgrim.

He hadn't known about my leaving the trail or coming back so Pilgrim was surprised to find me kneeling beside his tent when he opened his eyes that morning. We talked for a long time there on the ridge, about all that had happened to each of us since Delaware Water Gap in Pennsylvania. His own trip seemed one of wandering inclination, trying to experience as many facets of the trail as he could with no distance goals, camping instead wherever the end of day found him. Planning tentatively to meet again later, I left Pilgrim and Chester and walked the easy trail toward lowland.

The N.O.C. is a privately-owned complex of buildings straddling the Nantahala River among twisted turns of mountain bottoms, along Highway 19W, near Bryson City, North Carolina. It annually draws thousands of people devoted to white water boating. The AT passes directly through the camp and nearby bunkhouse space was provided me for $11.50, with kitchen privileges and a shower thrown in.

The availability of food supplies at the outfitter's store wasn't great but I didn't need much; other stops were available not far down the trail. At a communal center in the middle of the bunkroom and cabin cluster were restrooms and showers with an upstairs kitchen and dining area. A local high school had provided free snacks to hikers coming through, but most of that had been eaten by the two young northbound men I met there.

After resupplying and taking care of my equipment I loafed, with stops at the restaurant along the river where I could take in the practice runs of kayakers among the rocks below, and shoppers all around me emerging from one building to enter another. It was an ant colony of activity. I could only wonder how it must be during the peak of the season. Many of the people there seemed to be ordinary tourists, stopping for the panoramic background, but because there are no shopping strips or entertainment such as at Gatlinburg, I supposed most had come for the white water boating experience.

In the afternoon I stumbled across Pilgrim again and we continued our earlier conversation. He then left to send a package home and I went back to the restaurant. Pilgrim was unsure about whether he would stay the night at N.O.C. or walk to a nearby shelter. From my outdoor table I later saw him at a distance cross the highway and find the white blazes that marked continuation of the AT uphill and south. Watching him go I felt the familiar pang of losing something. Not very unlike the day at Spivey Gap when the others were forced to continue without me. I had to remind myself that this time, I too was going on.

Next morning I caught up to Pilgrim camped near Morgan Shelter, and though I knew I might not see him again, decided to not disturb his sleep this time. I said goodbye to Chester, who was guarding the campsite as usual, and passed by on the upland trail.

I walked strongly after the rest and made good distance, crossing Wesser Bald with an observation deck that had been constructed from the remains of a fire tower, to arrive at Wayah Bald at 5:00 pm. The day had been sunny and warm but turned cloudy toward evening. I had passed three shelters in going for mileage and found myself between Cold Spring and Siler Bald lean-tos, about 18 miles from N.O.C., but had thought to camp beneath my tarp somewhere near the summit of Wayah. Dark clouds and increasingly strong winds changed my plans however, so I climbed the stone observation tower atop Wayah to inspect it as a possible shelter. The waist-high wall and partial wooden roof would have been suitable on a calmer day, but with a lowering temperature, high winds, and the certainty of rain, I decided it was no place for me. At the bottom of the two-story structure was a room with open window and door, but there seemed enough protection to get me through the night.

How a stone building could leak so much is hard to understand. I had heard the plop of raindrops sometime soon after falling asleep, but supposed they were at the nearby door. Only later did I feel the wetness, and with my flashlight, saw leakage coming down the walls and dripping from the ceiling. The situation had become hopeless; my gear was getting damp and even with the groundcloth pulled around my sleeping bag, it was only a matter of time before I'd be literally washed out of the little room. Quickly then, with flashlight clenched between my teeth, I stuffed belongings into my pack, slipped it over my arms, pulled on my poncho, and raced 100 yards down a paved walkway to some privies I'd seen earlier.

A road leads to the summit of Wayah, where for a long time visitors have come to picnic and admire the view from the tower. Consequently, two outdoor privies had been built, and one had now become my overnight home. The facilities were tall and strongly constructed of cement block, with just enough room in one to lay inside my bag on the groundcloth.

Strong winds blew all during the restless night and at predawn I found it had brought piercing cold. Slow rain beat against the poncho, then turned to sleet and snow as I found the path leading down the mountain. Bare hands became numb from the cold and the golf club a hindrance. Its cold metal burned as though on fire. To keep moving was the only option.

A half-mile from the summit I saw a tent pitched among trees along the trail, its fabric partially obscured by snow, and felt better that those inside had probably spent a safe night. At the tower the evening before I'd met three young men headed north who were concerned about two girls following. They waited an hour for the girls to show up, and one had even jogged back down the trail in an effort to find them, but they were eventually forced to go on to find their own camp in the remaining light. They'd asked me to relay a message, saying they'd gone on ahead, but I didn't want to startle the girls by approaching the tent while they were inside.

I crossed Siler Bald, a frosted meadow in early morning light, and ate up the elevations of Winding Stair Gap in my effort to keep warm by movement. But the rain had ceased and the air warmed enough by 10:30 to remove the poncho.

Along the trail a hiker had spread most of his gear and clothes atop bushes and tree limbs, and said he was going to dry them a bit before walking further. I had already passed one vacant campsite where wet clothing on a tree had been apparently abandoned, as though its owner might have left suddenly in the storm, as I did, to seek better shelter.

At noon, after walking a mile of paved road to Rainbow Springs Campground, I again rented bunkroom space and dried my own gear. I was glad to be someplace relatively warm (the bunkroom was unheated, of course) and where I could rest. I surely hadn't gotten much sleep the night before, and was tired.

I checked into the camp store where the office was and had hot chili, the daily special, then bought enough food supplies to get me to Neel's Gap, 73 miles away. The hot, needlepoint shower I found at the community bathhouse was a godsend. Two northbounders also there, but for some reason we didn't communicate.

Went over 20 miles the next day with an easier trail, up and over Standing Indian Mountain. Met Lucky Laura at Carter Gap Shelter along the way. She had been in the White Mountains the year before and we remembered each other's trail names from registers. We talked about people we'd both met and it felt like old times again. This thing about meeting people from the previous season on the trail was, it seemed, bringing me closer to the old feeling of community we'd shared back then.

As I walked without conscious thought about what I was doing, tunes continued beating through my mind. The aberration had begun almost from the first, way back north. Songs would play over and over, like a loop of recorded tape, driving me almost frantic at times with their repetition. I was afraid it was only me until I heard other hikers complaining about the same thing. I wonder if it may be brought on by the cadence of walking with no distractions. In Georgia one hiker became angry at another for just mentioning a song title, knowing the tune would stay with him for hours, if not days. In Vermont I came from heavy forest onto an open meadow one morning in the rain. But soon, when the clouds blew away and the sun appeared, I walked through wet grass with a warming breeze in my face and passed an apple tree with ripened fruit, the hills ahead tinted with golden yellow light. Inspired, I began singing, "Oh, what a beautiful morning," and the song stayed with me for days, finally disappearing with the miles, much to my relief. Then, in January, while on crutches, my wife and I attended a revue of Rodgers and Hammerstein show tunes, and featured, of course, was, Oh What a Beautiful Morning, from Oklahoma. The song would then haunt me for days on end when I returned to the trail.

Sometime during the morning of the next day I crossed into Georgia, my 14th and last state of the trail. How many years ago was it I had climbed Katahdin, so anxious to begin?

Among the hills I occasionally heard what I had taken to be the distant noise of construction. It began as a low thrum....thrum...thrum..thrum, thrum—increasing in volume and tempo, like a motor beginning to catch. It was some time before I remembered from a television program that the noise was part of the mating ceremony of the ruffed grouse as they beat their wings toward the ground. It was remarkable how far the sound could carry.

At Dick's Creek Gap next day I wasn't sure about detouring to the Blueberry Patch Hostel, though countless northbounders had emphatically told me I had to go there. The place, they said, was "unbelievable." With 16.5 tough miles behind me I was tired enough for a rest but the Patch was several miles off the trail. As I stepped from the woods to where the trail crossed the highway, I saw an approaching truck headed the right way and, suddenly inspired, held out my thumb. Simultaneously, a hiker appeared from the opposite side of the highway and made the same motion with his left hand. Then, since the truck stopped, a decision had been made. I was going to join the northbounder in a ride to the hostel.

The Blueberry Patch is a small organic farm near Hiawasee, Georgia with space in a converted garage for hikers and was everything I'd heard it would be—great hospitality, softer beds, laundry service that provided clean, folded clothes, and a friendly homecooked breakfast for $15.00. I spent a pleasant evening there with three others going the other way, and next morning the owner took us back to trailhead.

Throughout the day, in addition to the ever-present mountains, I negotiated eight different gaps. Because it's always necessary, after descending the not-too-steep slopes, to climb back up to altitude, gaps are tiring. Especially when there are so many of them together. I met section-hikers who told of a shortcut, so I wouldn't have to "climb a couple of steep mountains up ahead," but I declined their instructions, saying, "I've come this far, I guess I'll go ahead and climb those, too."

Ever since Spivey Gap, it seemed, hikers had warned me about the mountains of Northern Georgia. But I'd been through Maine and New Hampshire and looked forward to the challenge, for comparison purposes, if nothing else. Then too, I was a bit surprised to find I'd become something of a trail purist on this last section, disdaining blue blazes and shortcuts. Perhaps because it would be over all too soon, I was determined to not miss an inch of trail if I could help it; was, in fact, beginning to savor in detail, every step I took.

With the late start from Blueberry Patch I didn't arrive at the shelter until 6:00 pm. Three hikers were there when I arrived, a married couple section-hiking and a well-built man, probably in his 30s, with hair tied into a pony tail, and a short-cropped beard. When I heard an English accent in return to my greeting, I said, "You must be Squeaks."

That he was, and surprised to hear me recite his trail history. I had heard so much about him from northbounders and reading his register entries I felt I already knew him. Like Pilgrim, he too had chosen to slow down, to delay the end. Squeaks lived the previous four years in Australia and began hiking the AT in August the year before, knowing full well that it was mid-season for doing so. At an outfitters he talked the owner out of a pair of ancient snowshoes used as a wall display, and continued through most of the winter.

At the Nolichucky River, near Erwin, Tennessee, he worked four weeks for a whitewater rafter, then with snowshoes strapped to his pack, continued south. Later, when the weather warmed, Squeaks lightened his load by selling the snowshoes.

So far it had been a cold spring for the south, but that evening was warmer and I wondered if the infamous skunks would at last make their appearance. A section in North Carolina and Georgia is known for skunk infestations around some shelters, and I thought balmier nighttime temperatures might bring them out. But they never showed, and I never saw one along the entire trail. Only noted their odoriferous presence at Andover, Maine the year before.

Most hikers seemed to have one peculiarity or specialty that made them stand out, and Squeaks' seemed to be the cowboy coffee he made that evening by simply dropping grounds into boiling water, then taking his pot from the fire and letting everything settle to the bottom. I drank directly from the pot when he offered it, and while it was strong enough to serve as paving material, I thought it the best unexpected treat since the camping leftovers at Fingerboard Shelter in New York.

That evening a full moon rose about where the morning sun would be and we all noticed that it seemed to balance on one of the nearby peaks. Next morning we were all awake in time to watch the sun first brighten the tops of the mountains, then bathe the trees around the shelter with slatted rays of light. Had I the power to choose an ideal day on the trail, that morning would be part of the pattern. But the rain, the cold, the snow and wind—everything I'd come through provided a total experience, and I would not have it otherwise.

After leaving Squeaks at the lean-to that morning I moved from being the last southbounder of '95 to the first southbounder of '96. I seemed to be having a hard time finding a place to belong.

I saw three hummingbirds that day, the only ones I'd noticed on the entire trip so far. But birds in general were numerous. I cannot imagine a good day without them.

My hike took me to the Walasi-Yi Center, an outfitter along highways 19 and 129, near Blairsville, Georgia. The trail passes directly through the center, making it a convenient stop for thru-hikers, with a downstairs bunkroom and a kitchen for overnight stay. It struck me as very strange that this would be my last supply stop. Just 30.8 miles to Springer Mountain, 2,131 from Katahdin.

Among hikers in the bunkhouse that evening were those concerned about heavy packs. They wondered aloud at the size of my pack that then weighed 22 pounds, and I eventually emptied everything piece by piece to show how a minimalist survived. One explained that he didn't want to know what I had, but rather what I didn't have. I had learned from experience though, that most hikers don't want to hear that. They have a way, at times, of becoming strangely attached to their belongings, however weighty and cumbersome.

Increasingly, those I met at the southern end seemed excited about my having come so far; the possibility of actually finishing the long Appalachian Trail must have encouraged them. While I envied them their future discovery, I was saddened to know that statistically, just about 10% of them would actually finish. It was impossible not to look into each face and wonder about their future.

I stayed long enough next morning for a final visit to the store inside the outdoor center, and to wish good luck to the hikers I'd shared the room with. Across the highway from Walasi-Yi the trail went steeply up and over Blood Mountain then down into Slaughter Gap. From there I walked over rounded hilltops and into more gaps. Again I felt the exhilaration of being in top condition. It was great to have everything working so efficiently again.

With the later-than-usual start I still made nearly 15 miles and arrived at Gooch Gap Shelter at 3:30, to share it with a man and wife section-hiking. They congratulated me on my progress and offered to share their food, but my mind, for a change, was on other things, and I declined.

The next day clouds gathered as I walked the path that took me among thick, dark undergrowth and past Long Creek Falls that with roaring, crashing water onto the rocks, was counterpoint to the silence of the forest. Along Stover Creek, past virgin hemlocks towering beside the path, I roamed. It seemed this next to last day on the long trail would be a microcosm of all the magic I'd found along the way, and a combined feeling of freedom and sorrow walked with me.

At Stover Creek Shelter I paused briefly and examined all the supplies left behind by overpacked northbounders, but needed nothing so near the end. I then trailed up switchbacks, finally gaining altitude after the long walk along bottom land. I had decided long before that, if the weather was fair, I'd camp in the open my last night on the trail— to watch the stars again and commit them to memory for a long time to come. But by the time I reached the top of Springer Mountain in early afternoon thunder had reverberated, it seemed, from behind every surrounding peak.

I dropped my pack and rummaged to find the golf ball carried all the way from Maine—ever since buying it at that little store in Stratton. I would spend the night on this mountain and save the actual ending of my trek for morning, but now, finding an appropriate rise with a tuft of grass to hold it, I reversed my walking stick and with 2,158 miles behind the swing, hit the ball cleanly, back north from where I'd come. I watched as it hung suspended for a moment in the gray-clouded sky, just above the deep, dark color of forest, until slowly fading from sight. I had planned the occasion long ago as a finale to my journey, should I complete it, but now saw it as something more. If I ever decided, in years to come, that I needed to do the trail again, I might attempt it this time south to north by chasing that little ball that lay somewhere behind me now.

From where I stood it was just over 1,000 feet to trail's end where the final marker lay embedded in rock. But for now, with feelings of both satisfaction and a sense of loss battling for control of my emotions, I had finally climbed the last mountain of the trail.

I stowed my gear in a small overhead sleeping area of the shelter and answered questions from a tenderfoot about equipment and the joys and perils of hiking, but my heart wasn't in the discussion. Three others arrived for the night but I had the loft to myself as I lay listening to rain sweep over the mountain to beat against the roof over my head.

Later, the rain stopped and it began to clear. I opened small window coverings that swung inward at each end of the loft with views to both the east and west. At one end I could see the newly-waning moon just begin to rise over a small lake, and at the other the sun was leaving behind a reminder of days passed.

I would leave at first light next morning and walk to the plaque marking the official end of the trail. I'd be alone as I bent to touch it, remembering in a rush, all the steps that had brought me to that place—all the events and people along the way. There would be no one to photograph the occasion or offer congratulations (only later would two of my brothers meet me at Amicalola Falls State Park). My arrival at trail's end wouldn't be the climactic celebration I had pictured all those nights in shelters along the way. And during the remaining eight-mile walk and arrival at the park's visitor's center, I'd strangely feel no sense of completion. That lack of closure would haunt me until I began to understand the gift: that if the trail never ended in spirit then I could perhaps retain all the journey had given me. Inevitably, I believe, all who walk the length of the trail must change. As miles passed the people I walked with appeared to develop an appreciation for the simple, essential things of life, brought on by knowing each day what is truly important in reaching their goal.

The trail is just that—only a trail. It was the journey that mattered and I think of it nearly every day. It ripples outward in the pool of my memory, touching, I'm certain, everything I am or will ever be. Because of it the world itself has become a better place. I discovered beauty and calm among the landscape of America and found for myself what was real. I learned to complete those things that needed doing, and I became more patient. Little things unnecessary for survival were no longer nagging problems.

Innate kindness and a helping hand from people both on the trail and along it reaffirmed a faith and hope in mankind, and that was perhaps, the greatest gift of all.

I would take with me all those things and attempt to base the remainder of my life on their belief. But for now I had the evening sky, and sat alone in my mountain aerie as shadows surrounding me merged with distant trees and the silence of evening expanded. I watched from my island in a lonely universe of reflected wonder as moonlight danced at water's edge; stayed while a million campfires died in the western sky, and the world became a deep, blue river in time.

END

Annie and the Salesman near Max Patch, North Carolina

LATER STEPS

I had no intention of writing a book about a thru-hike of the Appalachian Trail when I began the journey. Instead, I had an idea for a novel that I hoped to outline in my mind as I walked. It was probably somewhere around Vermont that I realized I was involved in an adventure more poignant—at least to me—than any work of fiction I was then capable of writing. As a matter of journalistic habit, I suppose, I had begun making brief notes at night, wherever I camped, and it was from those notes that I began this book while recuperating from the broken ankle in late '95. The manuscript could not be finished, of course, until completing the trail in May of '96.

Reading those notes and putting it all down on paper recreated for me the entire five-plus months the trip required. I was usually able to record no more than one day at a time because so many small details came flooding back. Each event I remembered then evoked another memory, and it often became too much. I would recall scenes that in and of themselves were spectacular to behold, but when compiled with all other events and feelings, my emotions just couldn't handle it all.

I am glad I have put it into writing and into book form. Not to justify my own efforts but for all those who shared with me the dream-come-to-life, and those who may not have the time or inclination to do it for themselves.

Fifty names were collected on the petition I sent to Ben & Jerry's. I could have gotten more but sometimes forgot to mention it when meeting other hikers along the way. No matter, I suppose. It was all for fun anyway. A copy of the petition was sent and a reply received. They said they would pass the suggestion along to their "alchemists."

Q-Tip stays in touch. As of this writing he lives with Max in Nashville, Tennessee and is engaged to be married in October of this year. He hopes to be able to move near the Asheville, North Carolina area some day soon, as he and his future bride share a love of the outdoors that could only have been heightened for him by the AT hike.

I hear from Laughing Gym, who does live near Asheville. He said he and his father have purchased a 40-acre farm there and he plans to provide a living with it.

Clarence is at this time involved in a coast-to-coast run from Delaware to California, via the American Discovery Trail. You may have heard about him by now. As of this date he is somewhere in Colorado. He has called and sent Email describing his new adventure. I admire the spirit in him.

Avi had moved to San Francisco and was working there, with a great view from a hilltop apartment, he said. Although I still haven't heard from Dixie, he and Avi had gone hiking at the Grand Canyon in '96, and then Dixie was said to be working in the ski country of Colorado. But he hasn't been heard from for some time now by any of the MEGA95 group I've been in touch with.

As of this writing Avi is planning a two-week vacation encompassing either a thru-hike of the John Muir Trail in California or a trek up Mount Shasta, then a 300 mile bicycle ride back to S.F. Either way, he says, he has to get back out there.

About seven months ago I got a telephone call from Energizer Rabbit from his home in Quebec, Canada. He said he hiked behind me from Virginia south, and did finish at Springer after I left the trail.

I don't know about Forest Hamster or Wandering Jack. Perhaps one day I will hear something. As for myself, I do miss the mountains. Since Springer, I have hiked in the Adirondacks, at Michigan's Porcupine Mountains State Park, and a part of the North Country Trail. In the spring of this year I returned to Smoky Mountains National Park and climbed to Chimney Tops, then walked the Rich Mountain

Loop Trail, gratified to find I could still do those things.

I know I will one day live permanently where mountains rise from the green-covered earth; where I am once again unable to see everything before me as I walk and there are things waiting to be discovered. A place where misty ridgelines lead past sweet-tasting springs to flowered meadows on open hillsides, and at night I sleep deep in my bag that in morning may be covered with frost. I will lie quietly there, a few moments more beneath a rising sun that only lightly touches the distant hills, listening again for the song of the wild birds.

Jim Coplen, South Bend, Indiana—July, 1998

Back home again in Indiana, November, 1995

EQUIPMENT

When it came to the things we were willing to carry on our backs, for myself and others on the trail, the basic thinking finally became, "If you don't use it every day, then you don't need it." That obviously doesn't apply to everything—medical supplies for instance—but it's a rule-of-thumb that could keep you going long after others have fallen by the wayside.

Boots, as stated earlier, may be the most important item of consideration. Agonies, too numerous to mention, can result from boots that aren't quite right for you. As a possible prevention of all that, I suggest visiting a qualified outfitter who can guide you accordingly.

Most AT thru-hikers wear out more than one pair of boots before they're done. I, and a couple of others I knew, used just one pair, but our slight builds may have had a lot to do with that.

Sneakers may look inviting, but I always felt my own feet needed the support of a stiff plastic or metal insert found in good quality boots. It seems to prevent a lot of the twisting motion that comes from boots without it. And believe me—the AT will twist your feet. I attribute my own blisters and sore toes—and possibly even the shin splints—to those cheap boots I bought at Bennington.

The choice of packs is a highly subjective thing, but I feel the more your pack can hold, the more tempted you may be to fill that space. The pack I picked up in New York had a capacity of just 2950 cubic inches. By any measure, that's small for long-distance hiking, but it worked. When I absolutely couldn't stuff anymore into it, I found I could always tie something to the outside.

Carrying a pack isn't simple—you don't just throw it on and go. Eventually we all found the right way to adjust ours so they rested mostly on the hips and snugged the upper back just right, but it's time well spent learning that before getting into the mountains.

I carried only a poncho for rain protection. Most catalogs and outfitters' stores carry a model that comes with an additional snap-out section that covers the pack you carry. It didn't necessarily keep me dry, but it held in body heat while I walked in cold rain, and it was much lighter than the waterproof rain suits others carried. Some hikers don't bother trying to keep dry while walking in warm rain, but always be aware of hypothermia. It often strikes when its victims are lulled into a sense of false security by temperatures in the 40s.

It's important, I believe, to always have something dry to wear when you're done walking for the day, and the new synthetics are nearly ideal for that. I always carried polypropylene underwear, even in August, because it weighed so little, and mountaintop temperatures at night could be a lot lower than anticipated. Other fabrics, such as Capilene, do the job at least as well. Fleece material is carried by many, for its warmth-to-weight ratio.

I had one pair of nylon shorts for hiking. If the weather was cold in the morning, I could wear the long polypro bottoms also, and change later as the day warmed. I also carried a pair of long, light nylon pants, (nylon dries very fast) mostly for wearing while in town or at the campsite, and an unlined nylon jacket that could be folded into a very small package.

At Waynesboro, Virginia, I had bought a long-sleeved rayon shirt to wear over a tee-shirt, and later at Big Island, bought the cotton jersey that lasted until November 4.

Two tee-shirts were always carried, alternating when one was too grimy to wear again. When both became uncleanable, I trashed them and got more.

A survival blanket—those things with a reflective coating—served as a groundcloth both in the shelter and inside a tent. A tarp, which was a little lighter than a tent, was used for shelter in warmer weather.

My sleeping bag at first was a summerweight, then

replaced by a warmer, 20-degree bag, but the lightest of its type I could find. I carried no sleeping pad, but almost everyone else did.

I carried one 2-quart aluminum pot for both cooking and eating. I drank hot tea or chocolate from one of the water bottles.

Essentials included a small plastic-cased flashlight, a small candle, medium-sized folding knife, about 30 feet of nylon rope, a set of nail clippers, and matches or a disposable lighter; aside from the food and stove that are mentioned elsewhere. A plastic spoon for eating, soap, and a towel. I also carried thermal glove liners and a knit cap in cold weather.

Two pairs of hiking socks made of heavy synthetic material protected my feet, and I always tried to keep one pair dry for wearing inside the sleeping bag on cold nights, even if it meant putting on damp ones in the morning. One pair of the light liner socks was enough as I could wash them out at night and they'd usually dry by morning.

A large garbage bag covered my pack when I slept in the tent or under the tarp, and of necessity were the two heavy duty, 16-ounce water bottles (In drought conditions I also carried a Gatorade bottle I'd found). Others carried larger containers, but there's a theory that the less weight carried, the faster you can travel, and the more water you'll find. One of the bottles is also a handy place to wrap a length of duct tape, good for all manner of mending jobs.

My medical supplies, after I'd become a minimalist, consisted only of two or three Bandaids, some ibuprofen tablets, and the ever-present Ace bandage. The theory I'd developed was that if serious injury occurred, I'd have to get into town quickly anyway.

A considerable amount of the gear I saw being carried by others seemed unnecessary to me and to others I talked with. The point is: all you really need is what it takes to survive under most extremes of weather that may arise, and probably will somewhere on the long-distance trail in mountain country.